OUR FATHER'S
VOICE

A Holocaust Memoir

To Tyeshia with my
best wishes for a great
life.

Felicia Graber
Nov. 15, 2023

OUR FATHER'S
VOICE

A Holocaust Memoir

COMPILED, TRANSLATED AND EDITED BY

FELICIA GRABER AND DR. LEON BIALECKI

♥

FOREWORD BY
KENNETH JACOBSON
Author of *Embattled Selves*

Our Father's Voice, A Holocaust Memoir

Portions of the historical notes in this book are reproduced with permission of the Holocaust Education & Archive Research Team (H.E.A.R.T), www.Holocaust ResearchProject.org; and Yale University Press.

Parts originally appeared as the essay "And She Lived Happily Ever After" from *And Life is Changed Forever: Holocaust Childhoods Remembered*, edited by Roert Krell and Martin Glassner, Copyright © 2006 Wayne University Press, with permission by Wayne State University Press and in *Amazing Journey, Matamorphosis of a Hidden Child by Felicia Graber*, Copyright © 2010 Felicia Graber.

ISBN-13: 978-1478151753
ISBN-10: 1478151757

Designed by Nehmen-Kodner: www.n-kcreative.com
Printed in the United States of America

By Felicia Graber and Dr. Leon Bialecki
feliciagraber@earthlink.net
www.feliciagraber.com

To the memory of our parents,

To the memory of our family members murdered during the Holocaust.

To our children, grandchildren, and the generations yet to be born because

You are the only gravestone markers our murdered ancestors will ever have.

You are their memory.

You are their future.

CONTENTS

 # Foreword

When I met the man whom I knew as Andrzej Bialecki, I was in the fourth year of research into Jewish identity among Holocaust survivors, and I had tape-recorded the life histories of more than 250 people. What struck me immediately about Mr. Bialecki was his eagerness to undertake the demanding and, for most others, daunting task of recounting his experiences under the Nazis. I was used to sitting down with people who were ambivalent, frightened, who dithered, who might even ask me to persuade them that the pain they anticipated in the hours ahead would ultimately be justified by the contribution they would be making to the historical record. Not Mr. Bialecki!

Arriving at his home, I found that he had purchased a new tape recorder expressly so that he could make his own tapes of the interview, and he seemed to me impatient to turn the recorder on and to get started. And once our conversation did start, it went on for a very long time: no other interview I did during nearly four years of work yielded more than six hours of tape, but in four sittings Mr. Bialecki filled more than twelve. His stamina was remarkable, particularly in light of the emotional intensity with which he spoke. His face often turned red, and tears came to his eyes; there were even times when I thought that he had started out to laugh but had turned to weeping instead. Still, at the end of each session he retained the energy, and what I interpreted as the commitment, to offer a few glimpses of what he would be telling me next time, almost as if he wanted to make sure he had enticed me back for the following installment.

These interviews provided the raw material for what you will read here. They have been edited with great devotion over many years by the Bialecki children, Felicia and Leon—and also, I would say, with great courage. For Andrzej Bialecki's account is unusually full and authentic: thanks to his remarkable eye for detail, his unfaltering memory, and his extraordinary honesty, he left behind a panoramic view of Jewish life under the Nazis, and one that in no way shies from the moral complexity of the time. The account that he, Felicia, and Leon have given us is no simplified tale of heroes, villains, and victims, but a chronicle of real life, of flesh and blood. In his acute observations and straightforward judgments, Mr. Bialecki spared no one, least of all himself. He was uniformly frank about Jew and gentile, rich and poor, pious and nonreligious, cultured and uneducated. To him it was the action that counted, and while he knew as well as anyone that it could be difficult—and was sometimes impossible—to make an unambiguously "good" choice, he was not about to make excuses or to cover up, on either his own behalf or that of anyone else.

That Felicia and Leon have seen fit to pass on their father's story unvarnished is thus, besides a great gift to those who read it, a courageous act. In fact, I would say that their prefatory passages, so dignified and so forthright about their parents and themselves, reflect their father's brightest qualities and demonstrate that they carry in their own character a precious part of the legacy that he left to his family's future generations.

—Kenneth Jacobson, author of *Embattled Selves: An Investigation into the Nature of Identity through Oral Histories of Holocaust Survivors*
Washington, DC
January 2012

 # A Note to the Reader

We, the translators, editors, and researchers of this document—Dr. Leon Bialecki and Felicia Lederberger-Ślusarczyk-Bialecki-Graber—are siblings. Our parents' names were Salomon and Tosia Lederberger. In 1942, when our mother was smuggled out of the ghetto with Felicia, her forged identification card was under the name of Anna Zofia Ślusarczyk and Felicia's name became Franciszka Felicja Ślusarczyk.

When our father escaped from the ghetto, his forged identification card read Andrzej Białecki. After the war, our mother and Felicia adopted the Białecki name. Our parents kept that last name after liberation, as it was still not safe to be identified as a Jew. Later, in order to obtain passports and exit permits from Poland, our parents legally changed their names to Andrzej and Zofia Białecki, which is the Polish spelling. In Belgium it became Andrzej (André) and Zofia Bialecki. The spelling was then westernized to Bialecki (without the ł).

Thus our family name remains Bialecki.

 **Preface**

By the time Europe was liberated in the spring of 1945, six million Jews had been murdered. Historians estimate that the majority of those who survived were between the ages of eighteen and early thirties. They were the strongest, the ones who were best able, physically and emotionally, to withstand the horrible conditions of being in camps, ghettos, forests, or in hiding. They were also most valuable to the Nazis as workers. The first to be deported and murdered were the elderly, the infirm, and the children—one and a half million children—as they represented useless eaters and unfit for slave labor.

I was born in Tarnów, Poland, in March of 1940, a few months after the German invasion on September 1, 1939.[1] Our mother and I survived mostly because of our father's guts, initiative, and an unbelievable amount of luck. I am very reluctant to call this survival God's guidance because it would raise the questions, "Why us? Why did we survive?" and, "What do I have to do to deserve this miracle?" I am well aware that there is no answer to these questions. What I do know, however, is that our father's ingenuity and our mother's courage were instrumental in the survival of our nuclear family.

In June 2010, I published my own memoir, *Amazing Journey: Metamorphosis of a Hidden Child*, recounting my personal recollections, emotional turmoil, and stories I heard mainly from our father throughout my growing-up years. There were many details, however, that I did not know until I listened to Kenneth Jacobson's twelve-hour taped interview before my first trip to Poland in

---

1 Tarnów is a town in southeastern Poland, seventy-two kilometers east of Kraków in a part of Poland called Galicia with a large Jewish population in the 1930s.

1994. Our family will always be extremely grateful to Mr. Jacobson for making this invaluable oral history available to us and future generations.

On November 15, 1996, I started transcribing the twelve-hour long German interview and translating it into English, a task that took several years. My brother, Dr. Leon Bialecki, took it upon himself the enormous task of editing and streamlining the text.

I verified as many historical facts our father recalled as I could. My friend Felicia Wertz read the material, corrected the spelling of Polish names and places, and through her own research, as well as her vast knowledge of history, corroborated the historical events our father referred to. The footnotes reveal some of my recollections of events our parents recounted and point out some inconsistencies we found in the text. In addition, some chapters offer historical notes that complement and occasionally revise our father's narrative.

A short oral history from our mother, Tosia Lederberger/Zofia Białecki, follows in Part II. It was taped at my home sometime between Father's death on June 28, 1991, and her own passing on November 12, 1993. Her brief account, narrated in Polish, deals mainly with the years she lived alone with me on Aryan papers. Felicia Wertz provided me with an accurate translation of the Polish text. I am very grateful to Felicia for her help. Mother's text was also edited to make it more understandable to English-speaking readers.

—Felicia Graber

 # Introduction

In 1981, a young American journalist, Kenneth Jacobson, working in Paris, became interested in the Holocaust. Being fluent in German, French, and Dutch, he dedicated the next seven years of his life to interviewing 250 survivors throughout Europe. The result of this endeavor was the book *Embattled Selves*, published by Atlantic Monthly Press in 1994.

During his travels, he came to Antwerp, Belgium, known to have a sizable Jewish population including many Holocaust survivors. One of his interviewees referred him to Dad, who was more than willing to recount his Holocaust travails in a free-flowing narrative replete with flashbacks and laced with vignettes. We wrestled with how to faithfully capture Dad's style that is rooted in the Yiddish tradition of tortuous syntax. Undoubtedly, some of the flavor is lost in translation. We used our best judgment to shorten sentences, delete repetition, and add a nominal degree of grammatical discipline. Dad displayed an astonishing wealth of information, including names of individuals, places, and dates of events, many of which we were able to verify through published historical documents. As is to be expected, this is a highly emotionally charged narrative and, when appropriate, we describe Dad's emotional state.

We regard this narrative as an important historical document in the chronicle of the worst atrocities committed in the annals of human recorded history. Foremost, however, it is the story of our family and our father's legacy to be read and treasured for generations to come.

—Dr. Leon Bialecki and Felicia Graber

Tribute to Our Father

It took too many years to gather enough courage, dust off the old tapes, and listen to Dad's voice as he relives his Holocaust nightmare. Dad was obsessed with the Holocaust. He lived it daily; it always was there, till he sucked in his last breath. The Holocaust defined Dad. It was his destiny. The slightest association—a passing train, a particular face—triggered the narrative in a predictable Pavlovian response. His entire life appeared compressed into these fateful six years. They were the epicenter of his existence. Life's events either preceded or followed the Holocaust. Nothing else mattered. Mom, as most survivors did and do, distanced herself from all matters relating to it. She tried to block it out, to tame those demons. Not Dad. He unleashed the torrent, was consumed by it. He had no choice in that matter.

Only now I understand. Dad needed an audience, and my sister and I were readily available. Yet, I was a poor listener during my childhood and adolescence. I could not integrate the horror stories, which Dad delivered in excruciating detail. I could not endure his tears, the outflow of emotions.

Dad was a most unlikely hero. Before the war he exulted in the mundane and earthy. A bon vivant, he cherished the physicality of mountain climbing, of long bike trips. Evenings and nights were spent playing cards with his buddies. Alcohol was consumed generously. Not driven by success, he did not finish high school and had no pretenses of being an erudite. Nothing seemed to have prepared him for the impending onslaught. There were no hints, no indications that he would rise to such levels of heroism and moral grandeur. Circumstances propelled him to unimaginable feats, which he took for granted. At a time when much of humanity lost its moral and ethical compass, Dad raised his to splendid heights. To exhibit such moral resilience at times of unimaginable calamity, when such values were in short supply, is astounding. Tragedy aside, these were, to paraphrase Churchill, his finest hours. And when the war ended, Dad slipped back into his former self.

The enigma persists as to the remarkable transformation from a nondescript, hedonistically inclined, thirty-year-old pleasure seeker to a leader who spent as much time helping others as saving himself and his family. Why did he do these things? They were spontaneous and unrehearsed. They were a natural response to his deeply rooted sense of justice and fair play. Yet, Dad expected the same behavior from others when he needed help. He certainly was not hesitant in asking for it. Judging other people by his own standards and expecting the same proved deeply disappointing. Still, he would not have survived without some key people who offered their help; some had to be prodded, some gave it willingly. The identities of these "angels" fill the entire spectrum: Jews, Poles, Germans, Nazis, peasants, engineers, pious Jews, and assimilated Jews.

Dad was a risk taker, though mostly his actions were predicated on what he liked to call his belief in his sense of logic. His physical prowess and years of mountain climbing and other athletic endeavors undoubtedly were a factor in his leaning toward the daring. Yet, Dad's logic failed him more than once and was replaced by a sense of naiveté of astonishing proportions. Entrusting people with sensitive information, which any sensible person would have withheld, he endangered not only himself but also his wife and child. This apparent carelessness reflected his myopic trust in people. How should Dad be judged when providing shelter or compromising his secret address to so many people and thus risking his, as well as his family's, life? Heroic or irresponsible?

Dad assumed a sense of communal responsibility for his fellow sufferers. Was that an ingrained trait that never before was tested? He operated in a lofty sphere of moral autopiloting, his own ethical norm acting as the gold standard. The Holocaust was the great equalizer when it came to judging people's behavior, and many did not fare well. As humanity shed its veneer and disclosed it ugliness, Dad's own virtues rallied. The moral debris surrounding him spurred him to new heights rather than diluted his moral capacity. Dad found his raison d'être.

I have grappled with the definition of heroism. Was my father a hero in the purest form? For me, Dad's deeds must be placed in a unique category akin to those accorded the Purple Heart for action beyond the call of duty, such as retrieving wounded comrades under blistering fire. Dad was a serial hero who was driven by inexplicable forces.

This tribute would be incomplete without acknowledging my personal anguish for not having given Dad the recognition he so deserved. Why did it take me so long to grasp, or rather come to terms with Dad's bewildering feats? Was it because of my preoccupation with life's events such as providing for my family, coupled with indolence and the inconvenience of the subject matter, that kept me from delving into Dad's fateful years? I was a good son and proud of what he had done. But I stopped right there and did not possess the mental or emotional stamina to follow through, to picture myself in his place, to try to think the unthinkable. How would I have handled these ghastly situations day after day, week after week, year after year? Would I have succumbed to the hopelessness and the inevitability of certain death? Or would I have risen to the level of self-preservation and struggled to save my family and myself? And what about the gargantuan leap it took to save others in the same predicament? I struggled to pursue this staggering line of thinking, reminding myself that Dad was of the age of my two sons when he was thrust into this mayhem. I realize what I am left with is suffused reverence of Dad, which is weighed down by an unsettling sense of contrition.

After much rumination, a brewing thought surfaced through my subconscious, crystallizing itself into an outright epiphany: I could not undo the past but had to seize the presence and shape the future. Yes, I had let Dad down, but not all was lost. The tapes resonating with his sonorous voice were my salvation and path to redemption. They assumed a hallowed quality. Self-flagellation was not the answer. The answer was to let Dad tell his story and for all to hear it.

—Dr. Leon Bialecki

Tribute to Our Mother

Unlike our father, our mother avoided speaking about the Holocaust years. Just a brief glance at the number of pages of her oral history reveals her reluctance. Unlike her husband, she was neither the athlete nor the outgoing personality. She was content to let Father be the spokesman and leader. Yet, after Father literally forced her out of the ghetto with me, the two-year-old, she rose to the challenge and succeeded in maneuvering herself and me for two and a half years in a foreign and dangerous environment.

For Mother, it was very painful to remember those war years. Just as Father could not free himself from those events, Mother dreaded remembering them. After our father's death in 1991, I encouraged her to record her story. I did so very gingerly because, once she started, she could not stop. "It is like a film that runs inside my head," she would say, "and I cannot turn it off." Nightmares haunted her for nights on end following such reminiscences. One day, she did agree to record a brief summary of the years she spent after leaving the ghetto. She locked herself in a room and recorded a forty-five-minute monologue.

She did, however, love to talk about her youth in Tarnów, about her mother, her brother Ignaz, and her sister Adele. She recalled with nostalgia her school years, her involvement in *Hashomer Hatzair*, a Socialist–Zionist youth movement, and most of all, about the year she spent in Palestine.

Brought up in a strictly Orthodox Jewish household, she rebelled early against the many restrictions and strove to stand on her own two feet, not to be dependent on "anyone." Thus, in her late teens, she enrolled in a secretarial school, a step that meant mandatory attendance of classes on the Sabbath, which brought constant reprimand and scorn from her father.

After graduating, she worked as a bookkeeper for a large company, but her dream was to go to Palestine, to learn farming and join a *kibbutz*, a collective community that is traditionally based on agriculture. In 1933 she joined a group of young men and women making *aliyah* (i.e., the immigration of Jews to the land of Israel, a basic tenet of Zionist ideology) and enrolled in an agricultural school in the land of her ancestors. I think that year was one of the happiest in her life. Even in her seventies and eighties, she would often recall the dirty, strenuous work with love and nostalgia. She would describe her friends, her teachers, the summer heat, the dreams she had had for her future.

But, then, a year later, the telegram came. Her mother was gravely ill; her days were numbered. So Mother packed a few necessary belongings and made the long trip back home. She absolutely intended to return to Palestine. She knew that pioneer existence was her destiny.

However, life had other plans for her. She never did return. Her mother died a few weeks after her return to Poland; her sister died in childbirth a few months later. She and her brother were shaken by the severe, double blows. How could she leave him now when he needed her support and help? She found another secretarial job and remained in Poland.

On March 6, 1939, she married our father. He came from a relatively well-to-do family, and her future seemed to look up. But again, fate intervened; a few months after the wedding, on September 1 of that year, Hitler invaded Poland. Life would never again be the same. By the time I was born the following March, living had become a struggle. Each day new restrictions were imposed on the Jewish population.

It was after the second deportation—the deportation of some Jews and children from the Tarnów ghetto, in September 1942—that our father forced Mother to escape to the Aryan side to live on forged documents. This was just the beginning of a long and dangerous journey that would propel her into a new, perilous, and treacherous world where a wrong word or a wrong gesture could mean the end of both our lives.

I am not sure how our mother managed to blend into Polish society, to teach me the necessary Catholic prayers and train me how to behave in church. She had to create and assimilate her new family name and background as the wife of a Polish soldier missing in action and to drill into me these newly minted family "facts." Later, she would hide our father in the one-room apartment and, again, make sure I, the then three-year-old, did not divulge his presence. We are fortunate to be able to add her short narrative to complement our father's.

To conclude my tribute to Mother, I offer a few selected lines from a poem of admiration said every Friday evening by Jewish husbands in praise of their wives:

Aishes Chail—A Woman of Valor

A woman of valor, who can find? Her value is far beyond pearls.
Her husband's heart relies on her and he shall lack no fortune.
She does him good and not evil, all the days of her life.
She girds her loins in strength, and makes her arms strong.
She extends her hands to the poor, and reaches out her hand to the needy.
Strength and honor are her clothing, she smiles at the future.
She opens her mouth with wisdom, and partakes not the bread of laziness.
Her children arise and praise her, her husband, and he lauds her:
"Many daughters have amassed achievement, but you surpassed them all."
False is grace and vain is beauty, a God-fearing woman—she should be praise.

—Felicia Graber

PART 1

Salomon Lederberger/Andrzej Białecki: The Holocaust Years

Growing Up in Poland

I was born in 1909; so, I will be seventy-two years old in four months. I come from a middle-class family. My father was a watchmaker. He came originally from Poland, the part that used to be Austria-Hungary. I was born an Austrian. My father's family was very poor. As a young man, he went to Germany, and at first he earned some money as a door-to-door salesman.

When he felt mature enough to get married, he came back to his homeland (Poland) and married my mother. They moved to Żabno, where their three children, including me, were born.[1] Żabno was a little town with perhaps five or six thousand inhabitants; it is not far from the bigger town of Tarnów. Then, during World War I, my family moved to Tarnów. I was then five years old, and I remember walking there, since there were no other means of transportation. Slowly my father worked himself up. In the meantime, he had learned watchmaking and became a watchmaker. I had a sister, Rachel, who was two years older than I. She and her husband, Jacob Kresch, were killed during the war. My younger brother, Ted, was born in 1913 and died as a very young man of poisoning.[2] We did not have penicillin then; otherwise, he would have lived. Later on, I took over the business as master goldsmith and also as a jeweler and watchmaker. Well, this then was approximately my background and my surroundings.

My parents were religious. My father had a short beard but no *peyes* (side locks worn by some Orthodox Jewish men). My mother wore a *sheitel* (wig

---

1 Żabno is a town and municipality in southern Poland, fifteen kilometers north of Tarnów.
2 According to Dad, he choked to death. It was presumably a streptococcal infection.

worn by some Orthodox married women). Saturdays and Holy Days my father wore a *stramel* (a hat decorated with fur worn by some Orthodox Jewish men). He was religious but not a fanatic. He came from the West, and he considered himself more civilized and cultured. He had spent several years in Germany and had "brought along" the air of the modern world to the East. He was not a fanatic, absolutely not; he was very tolerant.

As a young man, I was not religious, but my father tolerated that. He would say, "You are old enough to know what you are doing. Do not play any games for me." I had joined a Jewish Boy Scout organization called *Hashomer Hatzair* (the Socialist–Zionist youth movement). This organization still exists today in Israel and in the whole world. I read Darwin's theory and realized that the Bible was unrealistic. I have always lived according to my logic, not by my emotions. To this day I follow the way my logic tells me. I ate *treif* (nonkosher food) but of course not at home. Our house was kosher. That's about all I have to say about the overall picture. I became a Zionist, was a Zionist, and to this date I am a Zionist. I am for Israel. I was always a Jew and will die a Jew.

As I said, my father came from a poor home. He started working as a very young man. My paternal grandfather worked in a brewery; his wife, my paternal grandmother, drove to the market with fabric, which at that time was not sold by the meter, but by the elbow (the length from the elbow to the hand). That is what she did, come summer or winter. In my father's family, there were three girls and two boys. My father had already a job at the age of ten. In those years when peasants drove to the city there were booths, and peasants had to pay a road toll. That is how the authorities paid for road repairs. My father had such a job working in a tollbooth. Everyone wanting to drive through had to pay; that is the kind of job he had as a ten-year-old boy.[3]

My father told me that as a young man he lived in Worms and Leipzig, as well as in many small towns in Germany, until he decided to come back to Poland. He came back to Poland because his brother-in-law was a watchmaker who lived in a little town called Brzesko, where he had come from.[4] In Yiddish

---

3 Felicia remembers Father saying that very often, the peasants tried to drive by without paying and would use their whips to drive our grandfather away.

4 Brzesko is a town approximately twenty-five kilometers west of Tarnów and fifty kilometers east of Kraków.

the town was called Briegel (or Brigel). There, my father learned the skills of a watchmaker. When he passed his master watchmaker test he married my mother and went to Żabno, where all three children were born. My sister was two years older than I. She was born in 1907. I was born in 1909, and my little brother was born in 1913, four years after me.

I started to work in the 1920s. I did not want to study. I liked to play, so my father said to me: "Listen, my son. I see that you will not become a rabbi or a professor. You do not like to study, so I will give you a profession as a goldsmith so that you will have something in your hands and you will be able to earn a living no matter where you will be; you will be able to earn your daily bread." That is what I did. I passed my master test and later on I worked in my father's store and eventually took it over.

There was great anti-Semitism in Tarnów. When I was in elementary school, which was a public school, the teacher never called us by name but always addressed us as: "You little Jew from the first row, come here." The other children picked up on this and teased us. They called us "you, *żydek*" (little Jew). It was not a friendly atmosphere, and there were constant fights. They harassed the Jewish boys because we were in the minority, and the teachers encouraged them.

I lived and worked in Tarnów when Germany invaded Poland in 1939. In the 1930s our ears were open as to what was going on when Hitler came to power and what was happening to the Jews, especially the persecutions. But Poland was isolated. It was very difficult to emigrate from Poland. In order to get a passport you had to be in a higher social class. In other words, you had to have money, in which case it was easier to get a visa and you could get to England or maybe to France or even go to America. My father was enthralled by the German culture. He often would tell me about it when I was a young man.

In Tarnów there were perhaps fifty thousand to fifty-five thousand inhabitants. The majority of the city was Jewish, about thirty thousand. As a matter of fact, the Poles were in the minority if you did not include the surrounding areas where the peasants, who were not Jewish, lived. In the parliamentary elections the Jews were the majority, especially if you included Kraków.[5] In Tarnów we always elected Jewish deputies.

Food products were unbelievably cheap. There was a marketplace where peasants came to sell potatoes, wheat, coal, and other goods. At the end of the day they didn't want to load up their horses on their way back, so they would dump their unsold goods in the middle of the square. But there were Jews who were very poor. For example, one Friday, we were about to close shop, and my father wanted to go home to get ready for the Sabbath. I was in the process of locking up the expensive items in the safe, when a friend came in to borrow some money. It was perhaps half an hour before the Sabbath. He said: "Leibisch"—that is what my father was called, though his Hebrew name was Leib Israel. His actual name was Leon like my son's—"I came to you, although I owe you already five *złotys* (Polish currency), but I have no way out. I did not want to come. I was hoping that something would come in. People say that ten minutes before *Shabbos* (Yiddish for "Sabbath") it is not yet *Shabbos*. I was hoping that something would come in, but I have no bread for my family." My father loaned him money. After the man left, I asked my father how it was possible that he was so poor. I knew the man had a wheat business; so, how could he have no bread for his family? My father said to me, "You little fool. He goes to peasants and takes a sack of wheat on commission to sell and makes in the deal one half of a *złoty*. He has no grain in the house. He owes money everywhere. He has four or five children." There was unbelievable poverty among the Jews as well as among Poles. Often a decision had to be made between a piece of bread and wood to heat the house. That is how things looked in Poland.

---

5 Kraków is the second largest and one of the oldest cities in Poland.

🗐 Historical Notes

Poland. The website www.worldfacts.us offers this brief history of Poland: "Poland is an ancient nation that was conceived near the middle of the 10th century. Its golden age occurred in the 16th century. During the following century, the strengthening of the gentry and internal disorders weakened the nation. In a series of agreements between 1772 and 1795, Russia, Prussia, and Austria partitioned Poland amongst themselves. Poland regained its independence in 1918 only to be overrun by Germany and the Soviet Union in World War II." World Facts, "Facts About Poland," http://www.worldfacts.us/Poland.htm.

Tarnów. The city of Tarnów plays a very important role in our family history; not only was Felicia born there, but so were our mother and her two siblings. Our paternal grandparents moved their family to Tarnów during World War I, and our grandfather established a successful watchmaker and jewelry store on the city's main thoroughfare, Krakowska Street.

Tarnów Jewish community. According to *The Yivo Encyclopedia of Jews in Eastern Europe*, Jews played an important role in the city's commerce. "The community numbered around 25,000, or 40–45 percent of the population, at the outbreak of World War II in1939." *The Yivo Encyclopedia of Jews in Eastern Europe*, vol. 2, edited by Gershon David Hundert (New Haven, CT: Yale University Press, 2008), 1847–48).

The publication *In Your Pocket Essential City Guides: Tarnów* notes that the city's Jewish history dates back to the fifteenth century. Jews "were first mentioned in the city in 1445 … [and] they were granted the rights to establish a place of worship in the sixteenth century. … In October 20, 1939, Tarnów was the first city in Poland where Jews were forced to wear Star of David armbands." "Jewish Tarnów," http://www.inyourpocket.com/poland/tarnow/sightseeing/jewish-tarnow.

The Clouds of War

I got married in 1939 in the beginning of March. The Germans threatened the Danzig corridor and marched into Czechoslovakia and Vienna. But we were stuck. We could not leave the country. Besides that, we had parents to take care of and we had faith. We did not know yet that every Jew would have a death penalty over his head, as well as anybody of Jewish descent. Life was still relatively normal. I worked with my father. My father's business was in my name because my father had retired due to his rheumatism and pain. Besides, the internal revenue officials squeezed out every penny from the Jews. It was actually a persecution. I remember there were always inspections in the store. The Polish authorities demanded that my father be placed in a higher tax category. Tax rates were determined by categories. There were ten or twelve tax categories, number one being the highest. Every year one had to buy a so-called professional card in order to be allowed to work. They put pressure on my father to change from the third to the second tax category. In the second category you had to keep books and hire a bookkeeper. The bookkeeping had to be open for inspection. They made surprise inspections, checked the inventory and the books. Our business, however, could not afford another employee such as a bookkeeper. The taxes were exorbitant. (Władysław) Grabski was the finance minister and he squeezed out every penny from the Jews. So in 1939, when I got married, my father said, "You know what. Take over the store. I don't want to have anything to do with the government anymore or with the finance agency. It is going to be a new store on a new name, and I will come in and will help out, of course. We will work together." He did come in to help out, but the business was registered under my name.

My wife was five months pregnant when the Germans overran Poland. My friends wanted to flee to the East, and they came to me, wanting we should go along. My wife wanted to have an abortion so that we would be able to join them. She even went to the doctor to have an abortion. However, he said: "First of all I am not allowed to do it, and then any minute a bomb could be placed in the train station." We lived not far from the train station. The Germans had spies everywhere and sent them to sabotage railroads. The whole train station could blow up. They had put dynamite under the post office and destroyed it. The doctor, who was a friend, also said that even if he wanted to do an abortion, the electricity could go out any minute and therefore he could not do it.[1] Another friend, also a physician, claimed that my wife could do the journey East in the fifth month. There were no means of transportation, neither by train, car, nor horse. The Polish army had confiscated horses and every car in order to prepare for the war. They wanted to march on Berlin. The officers had left for war saying, "See you in Berlin!" They thought they would conquer Germany. But you know what actually happened. Poland was invaded without any real resistance. There were no weapons, no preparations, while Hitler had prepared for years. His motto was, "Arms instead of butter." For the Germans, the invasion was child's play. They just marched in. As it turned out we didn't flee; we stayed. First came the military, and slowly and successively everything started to become normal again under German occupation.

---

1   Felicia remembers: "Mother said that Dad's father also begged her not to abort, for religious reasons. Dad's parents were also very anxious to have a grandchild. Rachel, Father's sister, could not have children and Dad's brother had died as a young man. I was to be their first grandchild. Mother talked a lot about how my grandfather would come every day to see me as long as it was safe for him to go out."

🗐 Historical Notes

German invasion of Poland. The website This Day in History (www.history. com) reports that on September 1, 1939, "at 4:45 a.m., some 1.5 million German troops invaded Poland all along its 1,750-mile border with Germany. … Simultaneously, the German *Luftwaffe* (German Airforce) bombed Polish airfields, and German warships and U-boats attacked Polish naval forces in the Baltic Sea." Two days later, September 3, Britain and France declared war on Germany. *The Holocaust Encyclopedia* adds that Hitler and Stalin had signed the Non-Aggression Pact in August 1939, and "by a combination of German and Soviet forces, Poland was defeated by October 6 and partitioned between Nazi Germany and the Soviet Union." United States Holocaust Memorial Museum, "World War II in Europe," http://www.ushmm.org/wlc/en/article. php?ModuleId=10005137.

Lucy S. Dawidowicz, in her book *The War Against the Jews, 1933–1945* (New York: Bantam Books, 1978) estimates that the Jewish population of Poland in 1939 was "3,300,000 and that 90 percent were murdered" (544).

The Germans occupied Tarnów on September 8, and, as *The Yivo Encyclopedia of Jews in Eastern Europe* asserts, "immediately set fire to a number of Jewish buildings, including the Great Synagogue. … In May 1940, a number of local Jewish leaders were deported to Auschwitz." *The Yivo Encyclopedia of Jews in Eastern Europe*, vol. 2, edited by Gershon David Hundert (New Haven, CT: Yale University Press, 2008), 1847–48.

 # Assault on the Jewish Population

The Germans installed a German commander who issued various regulations to the Jewish storeowners: we had to keep the stores open; we had to sell all merchandise according to prices they set even though the money had been devalued. The *złoty* was not even worth half of what it used to be; later on, not even a quarter. But the stores had to remain open and the merchandise had to stay there; otherwise, you were punished, sometimes even executed. You gave everything away to the German soldiers—watches and other items. You hid as much as possible, but you had to have some merchandise available for sale. German soldiers would come into the store in packs of maybe fifteen to look at watches, and they would steal. For example, one soldier would show another soldier a watch, and then the watch would disappear. I could not fight them. We were open from 9 a.m. to noon and from 3 p.m. to 5 p.m. It was a plunder of Jewish businesses.

Then one after another, additional rules and regulations came out: Jews had to wear the Jewish star on the left arm; Jews were not allowed to walk on the main street. Slowly but surely, the Jews were humiliated and put down. Jews were not allowed to wear beards. The majority of the population was strictly Orthodox with *peyes* and beards; they had to cut them off. We were not allowed to walk on the sidewalk, but only in the street. Then, we had to give up all fur coats. That happened after the twenty-first of June when the Germans invaded Russia.[1] There were special places where we had to drop off the furs. Later, we had to give up radios. For everything, there was the death penalty. Jews were

---

1 The invasion actually occurred on June 22, 1941.

not allowed to have any flour but only *Schrot* (coarse, unrefined flour mixed with sawdust). The synagogues were mined and burned down, and the first shots were fired in the Jewish quarter. The quarter was totally Jewish; the only Poles living there were custodians. One day, members of the Gestapo walked into the Jewish quarter and began shooting wildly, killed sixteen Jews like wild-life, like rabbits.[2] In the next edition of the magazine *Świadek* (Witness, in Polish) that appeared in Kraków, they wrote that the Germans had discovered an underground conspiracy against the German rulers in Tarnów, that they had destroyed it entirely, and the leaders had been shot. In fact, they were just Orthodox Jews with beards and *peyes*. They probably were on their way to pray or to the *mikvah* (ritual immersion pool), and the Germans just shot them. The whole incident was turned around claiming that there had been an insurrection. So, the first victims were sixteen Orthodox Jews who were shot. That was approximately at the end of 1940 or the beginning of 1941. I did not keep a diary. The first deportation (of Jews to death and concentration camps) took place on June 10, 1942. That is when my parents and my wife's father were also deported.

We had the jewelry store on the main street in Tarnów (4 Krakowska Street). In the store, we also had a workshop for jewelry and watch repair. Later on, the order came that all Jews had to clear the main street. The main streets were Krakowska Street and Wałowa Street. The Jews had to disappear from there. We lived at 27 Krakowska Street, but my parents lived in a more heavily Jewish quarter (4 Franciszkańska Street). My wife and I lived in a fancier quarter, so we had to get out. This happened about a year and a half after the German invasion. There was a housing shortage. I moved to a small house with a big garden, which was located outside of town, after we were forced to move from our apartment on Krakowska Street. We lived on Gebniza Street for about one year. I got the house from our neighbor. He told me that somebody lived there, but if I gave him twenty thousand or thirty thousand *złotys* we could move in. Besides, rumors were that the area where his house was would become the Jewish quarter. Therefore, it was important for me to move there

---

2 The Gestapo, from *Geheime Staatspolizei*, was a secret-police organization that employed terrorist tactics against those suspected of disloyalty to Hitler.

and to live there. You could not get anything else, anyway. There were hundreds of people looking for rental housing, but no rentals were available.

Many people have asked me after the war, "Why did you not defend yourself?" since I was a strong, young man of thirty. I answered: "With what? With *shanes*?"[3] With what were we supposed to defend ourselves? With bare hands? It was impossible to fight against weapons and tanks. And the Poles did not help us; they betrayed us. Even friends just wanted to squeeze out of us whatever they could. There were rumors that Jews had jewelry and had millions of *złotys*, that they were bankers; and the Poles wanted to get everything out of us. The Jews were humiliated; they were put down like hunted wild animals, and the Germans kept on issuing new ordinances. They grabbed Jews and sent them to work. Nobody knew where to; that was a big secret. There were many ordinances, and if disobeyed, it resulted in the penalty of death. We were not allowed to use the streetcar or the train. The ordinances came out one at a time. There constantly were new ordinances; when a Jew passed a German, no matter the rank, even a simple soldier or an officer, the Jew had to remove his head covering and greet him. Some soldiers passed by without saying anything. Some stopped and said, "You dirty Jew, why are you greeting me? Am I a friend? You shit Jew, who do you think you are?" Another German, if you did not greet him, came back to you and gave you one or two slaps in the face or hit you on the head. Very few Jews went to the military before the war because, God forbid, the Poles did not want to Judaize the army. Therefore the Jews did not know how to fight. They only knew how to study the Torah, pray, and preserve the holy religion, the Sabbath, and the Holy Days. Under such circumstances, you did not discuss or even think about guns. Maybe in Warsaw it happened that they threw some Molotov cocktails, but that was later when we knew that this was a total annihilation. In the beginning, we did not know that.

I had to give up my store and workshop at the beginning of 1942. I rented a salami store even though there was no salami or meat available. A man gave it to me so that I could have a workshop there. My parents lived not far from this store.

---

3 On *Hoshana Raba*, the last day of *Sukkoth*, the Feast of Tabernacles, observant Jews beat the ground with a bunch of small branches, called *shanes*, as a symbol of atonement.

📑 Historical Notes

Jewish life under German occupation. The *Holocaust Encyclopedia* confirms Father's account of the conditions of Jewish life in Tarnów, stating, "[I]mmediately following the German occupation, the harassment of the Jews began. Many were conscripted for forced-labor projects, while others fled to the east. Among the duties of the Jewish Council [established in November] were enforcement of special taxation and providing workers for forced labor. During 1941 the Germans imposed a large collective fine on the community, Jews were required to hand in their valuables … and killings became more commonplace and arbitrary." The ghetto was also "surrounded by a high wooden fence. … Living conditions were poor, marked by austere food shortages [and] lack of sanitary facilities." Anita Stanislawska, *Private Guide in Kraków*, "Jewish Traces," http://www.cracow-guide.net/jewish-traces.html.

Jews in the Polish army. Dad's statement about Jews in the Polish army is contradicted in a statement by journalist Noah Klieger in his article *Army Was Polish; Soldiers Were Jews*, published September 11, 2006. Klieger claims that throughout the period in which Jews lived in Poland, many served in the Polish army, during all the country's wars and its battles. *Y Net News*, http://www.ynetnews.com/articles/0,7340,L-3302233,00.html

4

The Flour Incident

One Thursday, the following happened. Normally, Jews did their shopping for the Sabbath already on Thursday. They bought flour, sugar, and so forth. There was an ordinance that Jews were not allowed to use white flour and so my mother baked *challas* (traditional bread eaten on the Sabbath) out of *Schrot*. A woman came into the store and offered me a taste of some white flour. It was nice flour, just like a diamond. She wanted me to buy it. I thought, "My mother has such a hard time; she is not well, and we also have a small child." So I told her, "Fine, bring me five kilos," which she did.

My parents lived not far away, maybe five minutes' walking distance from the store, and I wanted to bring the flour upstairs so that my mother could bake for the Sabbath. I went into a passageway, which led through a house, in order to get to my parents' apartment.[1] A young woman came toward me and gave me a sign. I understood that there was a member of the Gestapo somewhere. So I ran up the steps, and as I got to the second floor, two members of the Gestapo stood just in front of me. I walked right into them. Under one arm, I had a book and the shopping bag with the five kilos of flour in my hand. I wanted to pass the men, but one of them said, "Stop, what kind of book do you have?" They always used the *Du* word when addressing Jews, which is the informal way.[2] He pulled the book from under my arm. Coincidentally, the author was a

---

1 Many houses in Poland were built with a passageway so that you could enter through the front door and exit through a back door.

2 In German *Sie* is the formal and proper way of addressing adults; *Du* is reserved for friends and children.

German who was born in Poland and spoke perfect Polish. The member of the Gestapo's name was Jung.

He read the title, "Sól Ziemni. What does that mean?"

I said, "The Salt of the Earth." It was a famous book.

"So, you are an intellectual?" he said and hit me over the head with the book.

I told him, "I am no intellectual. It is a story."

"And what have you here?" he asked.

"Flour," I said.

"Show me." So, I put it down and he tasted it and told me in these exact words:

"So, we Germans are going to eat dried-out army rations, and you will eat delicious flour. Where did you buy it?"

"Where I bought it? I do not know. Someone brought it to me. A woman came in and sold it to me. I have a sick baby who cannot eat coarse flour … only white flour."

"Where did you buy it?"

"I do not know," I repeated.

"You'll tell me."

"I do not know. A woman I do not know offered it to me, and I bought it." The staircase was made out of wood. "Lie down, lie down on the steps." There was a chair nearby. Then he took the chair and hit me over the kidney area. One time.

"And now you'll tell me?"

I said, "I do not know." So he hit me again until he broke the chair on my back.

In the meantime, my wife had come up; she did not know where I was. As my wife came up, he slapped her on the face and she fell. Next to the staircase were two long rods with metal hooks. They were used to climb poles to repair electrical wires. He took the two rods and again hit me over the back. Each time, I told him that I did not know who the woman was. Then he took a pistol and unlocked the safety lock. "And now you'll tell me or I'll shoot."

I said, "You can shoot me, but give me half an hour or an hour and I will find out."

He said, "It is now 4:30 p.m. I give you until 6:00 p.m. to bring me the name to Gestapo headquarters." The headquarters were on Urszulańska Street, number 18. "And God help you if you warn or notify them," he said, referring to the woman and whoever she had bought the flour from.

I did not know what to do, so I ran to the *Judenrat* (Jewish Council). I had a good friend and neighbor there and I told him what had happened. I knew the address of the woman, but I was afraid the Germans would break in and shoot everyone. I would be responsible. "You have to go to the Gestapo, but not personally. But first you have to warn the people. But don't go yourself. If you have a person you can trust, tell him to go and warn them that in case they have more flour in stock, they should get rid of it." I knew the woman by name and where her store was. She was the daughter of a wheat dealer. But I did not want to give it out, because I did not want to have her on my conscience. I knew the consequences. So I went to a friend who lived in the neighborhood and said to him, "Janek, here is what happened. Go there, but God forbid, don't tell anybody what happened. Just tell them so they are prepared." He must have done it because nothing happened. I could hardly walk because my back hurt. I had been beaten black and blue.

My wife told me to stay home and that she would go to the Gestapo on Urszulańska Street, where the Gestapo headquarters was. She would tell them that she came instead of me, because her husband was so beaten up that he could not walk. She later told me that she went there and what happened. In the hallway of the Gestapo headquarters was a window, like a cashier's window. A member of the Gestapo by the name of Nowak was seated there. She told him that Jung, the original Gestapo, had demanded the address of the woman, and she gave Nowak her address. She returned home. They did not detain her. A day or so later the woman came to us, as she had been told that the Gestapo had her name. She said: "God, you brought disaster on me." I said to her my life was in danger and that we had warned her. Anyway, nothing came of it as the first deportation took place a few days later.

📑 Historical Notes

In May 2010, Felicia contacted Mr. Adam Bartosz, director of the Regional Museum in Tarnów, whom she had met on her first trip to Poland in 1994, asking for information about the two Gestapo officers Father mentions in this chapter and about the location of the Gestapo headquarters. She received the following response:

> *Dear Mrs. Felicia Graber,*
> *On behalf of my director Adam Bartosz, I would like to send you some information about your questions.*
> *1) We can confirm that Gestapo headquarters in Tarnów were located on Urszulanska Street No. 18.*
> *2) About the Gestapo officer Jung. It is possible, that Jung could be a Gestapo officer in Tarnów, but we have no information about his life.*
> *3) About the Gestapo officer Nowak. Nowak Jan, arrived to Tarnów from Cieszyn, he knew Polish very well (but probably he was German with Polish sounding name – Cieszyn is city on Polish-Czech border, near Germany), he "led the investigations," he disappeared after the war.*
>
> *All the best.*
> *Janusz Koziol*
> *May, 2010*
> *The Regional Museum, Tarnów*

5

The First Deportation

A few days or a week later the first deportation took place. That is when my parents were deported and probably also the woman (who sold the flour). Approximately ten thousand people were taken away. My father was shot in the neck in the marketplace. Somebody told me that later. And my mother was also murdered, but at that time I did not know anything yet.

One more thing. My father was enthusiastic about German culture. When we still had the store, a friend of my father's came into the store. I was present at the time. He told my father, "Do you know, Mr. Leibisch, do you know what I heard? They took five hundred Jews in Kraków, put them on trucks, took them five kilometers outside the city, and let in gas, and gassed them all to death." My father became enraged and told him that that was pure imagination, Jewish imagination. My father said, "Get out of my store." Never in my life did I see my father so angry to insult someone. "Get out! I know the Germans better than you. They are incapable of doing something like that, and never come back into my store." He actually threw him out.

Later on, we found out that it was the truth. These were the first killings in Kraków, which was approximately eighty kilometers from Tarnów. Tarnów was a garment-manufacturing town, producing mainly women's and men's clothes and shoes. Kraków was a larger city of approximately one hundred thousand or more inhabitants.

A few days after the killings in Kraków, the Gestapo came to Tarnów. Everybody had to show their ID card, which they stamped. Some got the stamp with a swastika and some the "K" stamp.[1] There was a big barn, which was about two hundred meters long and fifty or sixty meters wide, and people were lining up to get the stamp. Meanwhile, a Jewish workers' union called ZTFA was established, of which a good friend of mine was one of the leaders. He gave me an ID card that stated that I was a metalworker because I did not want it to say goldsmith. Otherwise, the Germans would have taken me under their thumb. They would have wanted to know where I had hidden my diamonds and gold. So, I became a member of the union as a metalworker. My wife also received an ID card from that union. She was a "seamstress," and so she received the *Hochheitssiegel,* which was the seal with the swastika. At that time we did not know what that meant—what the swastika and what the "K" stood for.

On the tenth of June 1942 the first deportations began. There was still no ghetto. Entire columns of soldiers wearing helmets went from house to house and checked people's IDs. If someone did not have an ID with the swastika, which meant that he or she did not belong to the ZTFA union as a worker, he or she was shot on the spot or taken to the marketplace to be deported. My father had the "K" stamp. My mother did not go to the barn to get a stamp. Some people were shot on the spot, and some people were taken to the marketplace and transported to Bełżec, which was the name of the camp. Bełżec was a death camp. I found that out later on.

At first, we were under the illusion that they were taken to work, which is what we were told, that they were taken to the Ukraine or somewhere near the Ukraine-Polish border. I paid a railroad employee to find out what happened to that transport, where it went to. A week later, he came back and told me that the transport did not go to the Ukrainian border. Instead, everyone was sent to Bełżec and that nobody survived; everybody had been gassed. That is what he found out and he came to me with that information. Later on, I found out that my father received a shot in the neck. He had rheumatism, and the Germans wanted him to jump on a truck. But he could not do that. He was sixty years old, born on May 5, 1882. And so they shot him. This is a comfort to me

---

1 The stamp with the swastika was also known as the *Hochheitssiegel.* It was the desirable one, certifying that the person was employed. The "K" stamp meant the person was not employed, implying imminent deportation/death.

because he did not have to suffer like my mother. Millions of Jews had to travel that road of suffering.

The Germans were already on our street. We were lucky. We had the *Hochheitssiegel*, that criminal swastika. But they still came to our street and precisely at the house before ours. We watched, petrified, as they took a family, a man, wife, one son, and two girls in the prime of their youth, teenagers, sixteen or seventeen years old. The soldiers ordered the father and daughters to go out and not to turn around, and we saw how they shot them in the neck from two meters away. The mother begged them to shoot her. "Please shoot me," she begged. But the mother was not shot. She was an old, sick woman.[2]

Maybe they would have let us live because we had the swastika identification. The parents of these two girls did not have any identification cards because they were from Wyszyna; they were refugees.

After the first deportation, which was on June 10, 1942, a new ordinance was issued: All Jews had until the twenty-fifth of June to move to the Jewish quarter or ghetto. They published a map where the Jewish quarter would be. Whoever remained outside the Jewish quarter would be shot. As mentioned earlier, all Jews had to get out of the main street in the first half of 1941. We had moved from our apartment on the main street where our store was to the house on Gebniza Street, which we received from our neighbor. As it turned out, the house would not be in the Jewish quarter but in a different part of town, and so we had to move again. We had lived in that house for about one year.[3]

---

2 Mother noted, "We were only one house away from where the two girls, the father, and son were shot and we already said our good-byes to each other. Our girl played and there was only one more house between us and we waited for them to come to us. Then they checked their watches; it was already 7:00 p.m. and they terminated their 'efforts.' That is how we stayed alive. It was just an accident that we stayed alive."

3 Mother remembers that Felicia celebrated her first birthday on Gebniza Street.

🗐 Historical Notes

Bełżec was a small town located in southeastern Poland. In November 1941, SS and police authorities began construction of a killing center. Bełżec began gassing operations as a death camp on March 17, 1942. On June 19, 1942, the first phase of gassing operations ends at Bełżec after the arrival of over 11,000 Jews from Tarnów. United States Holocaust Memorial Museum, "Belzec," http://www.ushmm.org/wlc/en/article.php?ModuleId=10005191

The first deportation. Although *The Yivo Encyclopedia of Jews in Eastern Europe* states a ghetto was established in Tarnów on November 15, 1941, our family did not move there until June 25, 1942. "By then it housed 40,000 inhabitants, many were forcibly moved from surrounding small towns." That publication also mentions that the "first deportation took place between 11 and 13 June 1942 … when approximately 12,000 Jews were sent to their deaths at the Bełżec camp, another 6,000, primarily elderly people and children … were shot in the forest at Zbylitowska Góra, while 3,000 were murdered in Tarnów itself." *The Yivo Encyclopedia of Jews in Eastern Europe*, vol. 2, edited by Gershon David Hundert (New Haven, CT: Yale University Press, 2008), 1847–48.

Felicia notes: During our first trip to Poland in 1994, my husband and I found that clearing in the forest near the small village of Zbylitowska Góra. There are two plaques there, one commemorating thousands of Jews, the other eight hundred Jewish children murdered here and buried in a mass grave.

Testimony of an SS officer. The Holocaust Research Project website includes the powerful testimony of SS officer Josef Mueller, describing in detail his recollection of five deportations he witnessed: the ghettos in Kraków, Tarnów (first deportation), Miechow, Tarnów (second deportation), and Myslenice— although he is not quite sure of the correct name of the last one. Following is relevant parts of his statement. More excerpts are included following Chapter 8. You can find the complete testimony at http://www.holocaustresearchproject. org/ghettos/jmueller.html.

Statement by Josef Mueller
Former Commander of the SS Camps in Kraków

I have participated as an escort, in five such Jewish Actions with various SS-*Führer*. All these incidents happened during the period between March and June 1942. I had to accompany and take part, as a personal bodyguard, the *Oberführer* Scherner, on a so called Jewish Action.

[In June 1942] … we arrived into a town, which I was told to be Tarnów … In the ghetto there was once again a large square… On the square there were several police officers, I believe that a *Führer* of the SD, was there as well. The ghetto itself, was visibly, surrounded by police units. On the square were parked a large number of military lorries [trucks] … The driver and myself remained waiting … in the car … Whilst we were waiting, we noticed, that in the main road, the police lorries, which we have seen standing on the ghetto square, were being driven, fully loaded with Jews, out of the town, in fact, in the direction from where we came from, that is, in the direction of Kraków. After a short while, we noticed, these lorries returning empty. It was simply so that the lorries loaded with Jews, were being driven outwards, and the returning empty vehicles were driven back into the town. It was a continuous round trip… [After a while] Scherner [the command-ing officer] returned … [and ordered us] to drive to the German House in Tarnów in order to have our lunch there, and wait there for him… Whilst we were sitting in that German House, we could continue to observe the lorries on their round journeys… Hav-ing finished my meal, I have been curious to go into the street, I wanted to know what was happening to these Jews. After a few moments, I stopped a lorry loaded with Jews that was going out of town… I then told him [the driver], that I wanted to drive with him… We drove a short distance out of town, in the direction of Kraków … [where] there is a bridge. We drove over that bridge, and immediately behind that bridge, there is a field lane, leading off the road to the right. This lane led into a forest.

We drove into the forest. After about 100 meters the vehicle was stopped. I went out. The tailboard of the lorry was opened. The Jews descended. The entire forest was surrounded by police. As one entered the forest a little deeper, one came across a large opened grave. The grave was quite deep. The Jews, men, women, the old (no children) had to undress. In that manner they were led into that grave. They had to jump into that grave and lay down there. Down there in that grave there were two men with revolvers (probably c-8 guns)…

I assume that these men belonged to the SD… The Jews were made to lie down in the grave. They were then killed with a shot into the back of the neck, from the pistols of the two armed men there… Also over the grave, which I can well recollect, there were barrels of lime. A little further away there were several Jews working who were clearing up the clothing of their tragic comrades and throwing them onto one spot. This clothing was then taken back into town in those lorries. The lime had then to be thrown over the bodies of their comrades, by these Jews working there.

I watched these proceedings only for a short while, I became faint, I then immediately returned on the next vehicle back to Tarnów. Back in Tarnów, I had a drink of alcohol in a small pub… After a while … Scherner returned. We drove with him back to Kraków. During the journey no conversation took place, at least not about the liquidation of Jews.

There is also this other description on the same website:

On the morning of 11 June 1942, following a speech by Klee, commander of the criminal police, the SS men were issued rations of alcohol and they … armed with axes, broke down the locked doors of Jewish houses. Jews in possession of papers stamped with a "K" or with no papers were taken away or killed on the spot. Children were murdered by having their heads smashed against walls or pavements. Groups of Jews were dragged to a nearby forest and machine-gunned there; others were shot by the fence of the Jewish cemetery. Several hundred Jews were killed in the steam bath establishment at Czacki School, where they were choked by steam. During the "*Aktion*" 7,000 Jews were killed in Tarnów itself and in the Buczyna forest near Zbylitowska Góra, where they were buried in large pits. While these events were taking place, 11,500 other Jews were marched to the railway station, where they were loaded into railway trucks and deported to certain death in the gas chambers at Bełżec.

Holocaust Research Project, "Tarnow Ghetto," http://www.holocaustresearch-project.org/ghettos/tarnow.html.

6

The Jewish Ghetto

Now, we had a new situation. The Jewish Council created an office to distribute apartments in the area that was designated as the Jewish quarter. Many Jews lived there already and there were no possibilities to get an apartment. In the apartment in which we had lived on Krakowska Street and which we had to vacate, we had new furniture—a living room, a dining room, and a kitchen set—as we had just gotten married. It was a big apartment with four large rooms. We knew we would not have such an apartment again and that we would not need all the furniture. So we took with us only a big kitchen cabinet and a few chairs into the house on Gebniza Street. It was not really a house. It had one room and a kitchen and a big garden with fruit trees. Following the first deportation, after which we had to leave that house, we took this kitchen cabinet with us into the ghetto.[1] The ordinance was that all Jews had until 6:00 or 7:00 p.m. on June 25 to be in the ghetto. We came to the Jewish quarters in the last few minutes of the designated time, but there were no possibilities to get an apartment.

Thousands of people were pushing to get into the apartment distribution office where apartments were being given out. The Jewish militia had to control the flow of people trying to get into the apartment distribution center.[2] By coincidence, the main person in charge of assigning apartments was a friend of mine, a man by the name of Kuba Hier. He was a very distinguished man who

---

1 It is unclear how our parents were able to take a kitchen cabinet to the ghetto under these circumstances.
2 The Jewish militia refers to Jewish security men under control of the Jewish Council.

had been a director of a bank in a small town about forty or fifty kilometers from Tarnów. He had to flee to Tarnów because he was known to be a very wealthy man. But I could not get into his office; that's how full it was. It rained and it was already evening and we stood in the square—Resengrosser Square, which later on became the *Umschlagplatz* (the square from which Jews were deported to death/concentration camps). We stood there and in the last minute a friend of mine, Mr. Osterweil, who had arranged the identification cards for my wife and me, came out and said, "Schlomek, what are you standing here for?"[3] I said, "Why are you asking? I live here under the open sky." My wife had wrapped the child (Felicia) in a blanket and there was nowhere to go; every little hole was already occupied, every cellar, every basement was taken. It was impossible to get a room. So he told me, "Are you crazy? Come up to my place." He had a very large single room in the Michalewicz House.[4] He said that we would be able to somehow manage. He had two children, and we had the baby. It was 1942, so our daughter was already two years old. We took him up on it and we divided the room by means of the kitchen cabinet. My friend, his wife, and his two children lived in one half of the room, and I, my wife, and the child lived in the other half. That's how my friend saved us.

It was an impossible situation. People literally lived in hallways, since the ghetto was at most large enough for one-tenth of the Jewish population that had remained after the first deportation. Jews from all over town had to move here. There still remained about 20,000 Jews and at best there was room for about 1,000 or 1,500 people in this new Jewish living quarter.

And so life began in the ghetto. We were locked up in what the Germans called the Jewish quarter, but it really was a ghetto. We were under guard. Everybody had to have a job and work. As a matter of fact, everybody desperately tried to get a job. People imagined that those who worked for the military would remain alive and that only the weak, the old, and the very young ones would perish. We already knew what the deportation meant; we knew that it

---

3 Schlomek is the Polish form for Salomon, our father's first name.
4 The Michalewicz Workers Home on Ochronek Street was built by the socialist Bund party, which operated there. Tarnów - Jewish Historic Sites Tourist Information center http://www.it.tarnow.pl/index.php/eng/Worth-seeing/Tarnow/Jewish-Historic-Sites

meant the extermination of the Jews. So people paid the Jewish Council and begged to obtain work without pay. People even paid to work; they paid more than they could afford in order to work. Those who did not have money borrowed money. People paid unbelievable sums of money to work, though Jewish families were not allowed to own more than three thousand *złotys*. You had to deposit the money in a closed account in the Polish bank; otherwise you were punished. At first, it was not the death penalty, but later every little mistake brought about the death penalty. That is the way things looked until the second deportation. The conditions in the ghetto were impossible. A *Volksküche* (soup kitchen) was established by the Jewish Council in an attempt to feed some of the people.

Even before the second deportation, there were rumors of new danger. My friend (probably referring to Józef Fast) was a big fish in the Jewish Council, and he received a tip or warning of an imminent deportation from the Gestapo. My friend, God forbid, did not work for or cooperate with the Gestapo. The second deportation was carried out by the Gestapo from Kraków. The Gestapo from Kraków came, took my roommates, my friend Osterweil with his wife and his two children, to Kraków and sent them to a work camp called Płaszów.[5] Płaszów was a suburb of Kraków and was a labor camp. And so we already smelled that something rotten was going on. My wife and I became the only inhabitants of the large room, which was in the Michalewicz House. By the way, in front of the Michalewicz House was a kindergarten, since women had to work. Tarnów was a garment-manufacturing town and parents left their children in the kindergarten while at work. There, children were taken care of and also received food until the parents returned from work.

---

5 Mr. and Mrs. Osterweil and their two children survived the war. They moved to Israel where Mr. Osterweil had a clothing business. His son still lives in Israel, and Leon talked with him in 2009. His daughter, Zahava, died of a brain tumor a few years ago.

🗐 Historical Notes

The Jewish police and Jewish Council (*Judenrat*). The Holocaust Research
Project offers an excellent summary of these two organizations:

> Jewish Order Service police units were established by the German
> authorities in certain locations under their brutal occupation. Al-
> most immediately after their establishment the Jewish Councils in
> Eastern Europe were ordered to organize these units, usually as a
> forerunner to the creation of ghettos.
>
> Whereas the *Judenrat* itself, although also created on German
> orders, often contained elements of pre-war voluntary association,
> the Jewish police came into being only after the German occupa-
> tion. There was no precedent for the existence of a Jewish police
> force, and there was no indication that the Jews played any part in
> the establishment of a Jewish police force within the ghettos.
>
> The Germans set the guidelines for the *Judenrat* to recruit
> members which included physical fitness, military experience, and
> secondary or higher education.
>
> In practice these guidelines were not always closely followed.
> Formally the Jewish police constituted one of the departments of
> the *Judenrat*, but from the very beginning many Jewish Councils
> were apprehensive about the police force's public character and the
> way it would function.
>
> They suspected that the Germans would have direct super-
> vision of the police and use it for the implementation of their
> policies. Aware of this danger, many Jewish Councils sought to
> establish their own means of controlling the police and the stan-
> dards of its behaviour, and tried to attract young Jews who would
> be trustworthy.
>
> In the initial period some of the recruits did indeed believe that
> joining the ranks of the Jewish police gave them an opportunity
> to serve the community. But there were other reasons for join-
> ing. Belonging to a protected organization, provided immunity

from being seized for forced labour. Service in the Jewish police also offered greater freedom of movement and the possibilities of obtaining food and money.
Holocaust Research Project, "The Jewish Order Police: Holocaust Ghettos," http://www.holocaustresearchproject.org/ghettos/orderpolice.html

The SS. The official name of the SS Father mentions is the *Schutzstaffel*. As the Holocaust Research Project website explains, the SS "were established by Hitler to act as protection force at Hitler's mass meetings in public. Many of these meetings were violent and ugly, during the Nazis early quest for power. In the early days of the SS, officer candidates had to prove German ancestry to 1750. They also were required to prove that they had no Jewish ancestors It was the SS who ran the concentration camps first in Germany, then in Poland, with brutal efficiency, camps like Auschwitz which started its existence as a camp for Polish political prisoners, before being transformed into a dual death camp with gas chambers and crematoria and labour camp, where millions of Jews perished." Holocaust Research Project, "The SS," http://www.holocaustresearchproject. org/holoprelude/aboutthess.html

7

The Michalewicz House

The house in which I lived in the ghetto was named after the leader of the Bund, which was the Jewish workers' union, a Socialist union. It was called *Dom Michalewicza* in Polish (the Michalewicz House). Downstairs was a big room with a stage or a theater designed for performances that used to take place before the war. It had also been used for cultural exhibitions. During the war it just so happened that this house was located within the ghetto area. Even before the German invasion, there was a Polish ordinance that every house had to have a leader, a man in charge of the house who was responsible for putting out fires in case of bombings and for being prepared for emergencies. I was the leader of our house and had helpers. We filled sacks with sand and buckets with water to use in case of fire during the bombings. The same ordinance was kept by the Germans after they invaded Poland. My wife and I had the room all to ourselves, which was on the first floor (equivalent to the second floor in the USA). About thirty people or several families lived in the Michalewicz House. Adjoining this house was a low building whose roof reached about half a meter below my room. The roof of that structure was covered with tin tiles. In the middle of the roof was a chimney-like structure. It was not a real working chimney but used as an entry to a space between the roof and the ceiling of the rooms below. This space was used for repair purposes.[1] So I hired a sheet-metal worker—a Jew, of course—who was an acquaintance of mine and a neighbor of my store. He was somebody I could trust. I told him to construct a hiding place

---

1 The only way in and out of that space, or *Zwischenraum* as Dad called it, was through this chimney-like structure.

in case there was another deportation and people needed a place to hide. I had this idea, and since I was the leader of the house, I called him in. So he sawed down the structure and covered the opening with a plate of tin in its place. There were about three hundred of those square tin plates covering the roof so that nobody could tell which one could be opened and would lead to the hiding place. That is what I did.

And our suspicions became reality. German commandos arrived to prepare for the second deportation. They surrounded the whole ghetto with machine guns and so forth. And again we needed to get a stamp with the swastika, but this time members of the Gestapo positioned themselves in the office of the Jewish Council. There were thousands of people trying to get into the Jewish Council. People handed in their work permit in order to get it stamped. Some handed it over personally at the Jewish Council, but most could not get there and handed over their work permit to the Jewish militia. Some permits were stamped and some were not. We did not know ourselves if we would get the seal of the swastika. In Hebrew we say, "*Mi lehaim u mi lamaved*, who shall live and who shall die." The stamp would determine that decision. As I found out later, the Gestapo members made decisions according to their moods with no rhyme or reason. There was turmoil in our building. Everyone trembled; everyone was scared.

So I called together the people from the house in a big room, which we locked. Most heads of the families where assembled there. And I said, "Dear friends, please remain calm. I have set up a hiding place, and whoever doesn't receive the *Hochheitssiegel*, I will accommodate." And I told them, "But God forbid, do not tell anyone, not even a sister, because the space is limited for a small number of people." At most, I could accommodate thirty people. I took pains to calm the people down while everyone waited to get the seal. I myself received the *Hochheitssiegel*, which was brought by a messenger of the militia. It was said, and that was very important, that every mother, every working mother, could keep one child. Even if she had five or ten or three children, she could only protect one. I was calm as my wife and our child had received the seal, and my child was safe. We ourselves therefore did not have to go into the hiding place.

One late evening, it came to pass that two men came to see me. One was a wealthy and well-known architect, by the name of Haskel Hollender, and the another Jew by the name of Korn. I don't remember his first name, but that is of no importance. I told them that I had a hiding place that had to remain a secret; otherwise people would overwhelm me, and I could accept only a limited number of people. I told them that nobody except me and my wife knew how to get people into the hiding place. The entrance to the hiding place was quite small, so that only one person could slip through at one time. First, one had to go through the window to get to the roof. This had to be done only at night when it was dark; otherwise people could see that someone was going on the roof. One could do this only at one or two o'clock in the morning and only one person at a time.

In the evening, someone came to tell me that something terrible had happened. The entire hallway to the theater was packed with people (Jews seeking refuge): women, old and young, children, and men. I went down, and my head reeled.[2] Haskel Hollender, who knew that there was a hiding place, told me that his nephew was the assistant president of the *Judenrat* and that he was going to ask him to send in the Jewish militia to kick the people out. I told Mr. Hollender, "Listen to me. I am not the all-mighty God to decide who is to live and who is to die, and I forbid you to do this."

One thing we had to do immediately was to lock the main gate to the house, and then we had to find a way to accommodate the additional people. The people who lived in our house knew that there was a hiding place, though they did not know where it was. Word had spread quickly. They all had a mother, a sister, or other relatives whom they told that there was a good hiding place in the house. And they came with their families; the hallway was packed with perhaps 250 people. Yet I had room to hide only about thirty. So I decided to try to find and to organize a second and larger hiding place because we could not fit everyone in. I feared that in order to save themselves those left out would threaten to inform the Gestapo or the Jewish militia that there was a very good hiding place in the Michalewicz House and that many people were

---

2 "Es wurde mir schwarz vor den Augen"; literal translation: "It got black in front of my eyes."

hidden there, though they did not know exactly where the hiding place was. To protect the thirty people, I had to accommodate everybody. I told myself that it was wrong that, just because someone was not related to me or a good friend of mine, that person should die; yet if he or she was related or a friend of mine or my wife, he should live. I had to find a place so that all could stay. The three of us—Haskel Hollender, Korn, and I—went looking. There was no cellar. The room I stayed in was on the first floor. The person who built the house must have been a genius. It was a two-story house.[3] Above the second floor, there was a small attic. It was very small, just big enough to hang laundry, or perhaps they kept chickens up there. Right across from my room lived two young ladies from Kraków, two sisters. One was a virtuoso pianist.[4] Their room was very small as opposed to my room, which was quite large. In their room, I discovered an alcove about this high.[5] I saw a ladder in the back of it. I climbed up the ladder and I saw this huge, attic-like area that was the size of a double attic. I said, "Here we can hide all the people who are downstairs." There was a lot of wailing. I told everybody to stay calm. To the religious I was regarded higher than God. I was the savior. I told everyone to stay calm, that I had found a second hiding place and everyone would be accommodated. There were some complaints voiced that this hiding place was not as good as the other one. I told them that it was not true. I then looked for a very large dresser. Where I got it from I do not remember. We placed it right in front of the entrance to the alcove, so that all one saw in the room were a dresser and one or two beds.

The room that had the alcove leading up to the large attic belonged to the two sisters. As I mentioned, one of the sisters was a known pianist and was famous in Poland even before the war. Her name was Natalka Hubler, or Bubelle as she was known. Her first husband had been a lawyer in Kraków. After I discovered the alcove in their room, I said to Natalka and her sister, Helenka: "You have to allow people go through your room, because we can save about two hundred people—Jews." And they said: "That is out of the question.

---

3 Three stories in the United States.
4 Dad inserts that he met her in London in 1981. At that time she was still giving concerts on television and radio. Dad also mentions that he saw her sister in Israel.
5 Dad must have indicated with his arm how high it was. It probably was quite low; presumably to the waist or shoulder.

We are not going to allow ourselves to be placed in danger and be shot. We are not you." I thought what to do. In our house lived the vice president of the *Judenrat*, a man by the name of Józef Fast, whose mother and stepfather were to be hidden in our hiding place. The younger of the two sisters, Helenka, was rumored to be his girlfriend. He was also a good friend of mine and my bridge partner. So I went to him and said, "Józef, can you arrange for another room for the two girls, the two sisters, so that I can save some more people?" He said he would, and he was able to accommodate them. And so they released the room to me. I asked several people to move into that room, but nobody wanted to. They knew that there would be a hiding place there and that the first thing that happened when a hiding place was discovered was that the people in whose place it was found were shot. So I said, "OK, then, I'll take it. It is going to be my room."

First I took the people who did not have the proper stamp. Among them was a friend and cousin of mine who had come from Germany. His name was Grünkraut. His wife had received her stamp, but he and his two girls did not and needed a place to hide. That night, around one or two o'clock in the morning, I led people one at a time into the shelters. We walked slowly since the ghetto was surrounded by Germans. The deportation had not started yet. I took many buckets to be used for people's bodily needs. There were many empty apartments in the neighborhood since people had been deported, so that I picked up what was needed, such as buckets, pillows, and blankets, because there were also elderly people who were more needy. I also put there the furnishings of my wife. We were married in March of 1939, and the Germans attacked us six months later, so that all our furnishings were new. They still had not been used. We had received a bedroom and a dining room set after our wedding, so that we had all new linen, tablecloths, and new suits and outfits. They were all in suitcases. I had bought suitcases and hid them since I was concerned these things would be stolen.

Every night I had to carry the excretions, the feces and urine, out in buckets and rinse them in the toilet. Otherwise people would have choked from the stench. I also had an aunt there, Gela Verderber, with a ten-year-old boy in the good hiding place. They had come from Cologne. In the middle of the night I took her out of the hiding place to help scavenge for food. We went around the empty houses and whatever food we found, we collected. Not only I but also other people collected food and brought it to the hiding places. We had an oven and my aunt, who was a very good cook, made one big meal all in one pot, in order to feed the people for the whole week.

And so I accommodated all the people except for the very young children. I did not allow very young children because, I said, a child might cry and would be heard and then the whole hiding place would be worthless. On the other hand, I allowed children who already understood, say two or three years of age. But with babies, the only thing one could do was to smother them. As a matter of fact many little children were choked by their parents, because parents wanted to save themselves. Others just went with the children to their death.

So I was able to carry through all this during the entire night and by dawn everyone was settled in. When we came back to our room we discovered that an acquaintance of mine, whom I had not permitted to bring his child to the hiding place, had placed the child, a very light blond child, in the crib of my daughter.[6] My wife had dark hair, my daughter had dark hair, and there was this light blond boy. So the child just lay in the crib and we let him stay there. I later ran into the mother-in-law and sister of the mother of this child. I said that they would have to take the child and that he could not stay with us because my wife was dark-haired and that I could not keep a light blond, almost straw blond child. It would be immediately noticeable that the child does not belong to our family.

---

6 Dad inserts that this man and his wife were still alive as of 1981 but does not mention the fate of their child.

📑 Historical Notes

Natalia Natalia Weissman-Hubler-Karp. One of the two sisters Father mentions was Natalia Natalia Weissman-Hubler-Karp. She is listed in the archives of the *Lexicon of Jewish Musician in Poland* (p. 278), and in *Jewish Music in Poland Between the World Wars* by Issachar Fater. Both are available in the archives of the Jewish Historical Institute in Warsaw, Poland. Felicia read them when she was in Warsaw in 1994.

Natalia died in London July 9, 2007. James Methuen-Campbell, a reporter for the British newspaper *The Independent*, wrote in the paper's July 17 issue that she had been a prisoner at the Plaszów concentration camp in the suburbs of Kraków. Having been ordered to play the piano on the occasion of the commandant Amon Göth's birthday in1943, she chose Chopin's Nocturne in C-sharp minor—an intensely melancholic piece. Her performance moved the commandant who told Natalia that she and her younger sister would live. They were both freed from Auschwitz in May 1945. James Methuen-Campbell, "Natalia Karp, Pianist Who Survived Auschwitz," *The Independent*, July 17, 2007.

Gella Verderber (Ferderber). Father also mentions his aunt, Gella Verderber (Ferderber). That family's genealogy is available on http://www.familysearch. org. There were a Jewish and a non-Jewish branch of the family. Gella Verderber, born Rosenzweig, February 2, 1889, in Tarnów, Poland, was the sister of our grandmother, Sarah Rosenzweig-Lederberger. She lived in Köln, Germany, and was deported to Poland in October 1938, together with her eight-year-old son, Adolf Verderber. Both were murdered in Poland in 1942 or 1943. The Genealogical Society of Utah, microfilm no. 1573223, http://www.familysearch.org.

The Plaszów camp. According to a post on the United States Holocaust Memorial's website, the Plaszów camp, was established in 1942 as a "forced-labor camp for Jews."

In 1944, it became a concentration camp. Thousands were killed there, mostly by shooting. The German industrialist Oskar Schindler, featured in Steven Spielberg's movie *Schindler's List*, 1993, established an enamelware factory in Kraków, adjacent to Plaszów. He protected some 900 Jewish workers from abuse, and deportation to extermination camps. In 1944, he moved his factory and his Jewish workforce to the Sudetenland (an area formerly in Czechoslovakia) thus preventing the deportation of more than 1,000 Jews.

United States Holocaust Memorial Museum, "Plaszow," http://www.ushmm.org/wlc/en/article.php?ModuleId=10005301.

Another inmate at the camp, Joseph Bau, describes the conditions in Plaszów camp in his article "Journey Through the Past." It is available on the Holocaust Research Project website at http://www.holocaustresearchproject.org/othercamps/plaszow/bauplaszow.html.

According to the website www.holocaustresearchproject.org, **Amon Leopold Göth** was born on 11 December 1908 in Vienna, Austria. He joined the Nazi Party in 1932 and the SS in 1940. Drafted into the *Wehrmacht* (German Army) as a *Unterfeldwebel* (sergeant) in 1940, he was promoted up to the rank of SS-*Hauptstürmfuhrer* (captain) in 1944. In February 1943 transferred to Kraków as the Commandant of Plaszów Labour camp.

Prisoner Joseph Bau described Göth the commandant of Plaszów as follows:

"A hideous and terrible monster who reached the height of more than two meters… He ran the camp through extremes of cruelty that are beyond the comprehension of a compassionate mind – employing tortures which dispatched his victims to hell. … [H]e would rain blow after blow upon the face of the helpless offenders… During interrogations… he would set his dog on the accused, who was strung by his legs from a specially placed hook in the ceiling. In the event of an escape from the camp… he would, personally kill every tenth person" from the escapee's group.

Göth played a leading role in the destruction of a number of Jewish Ghettos, including the "liquidation of the Tarnów Ghetto… [where] he shot a girl who asked him for a transfer to a different working group to be together with her fiancé." He was arrested by the Americans in 1945, extradited to Poland, and hung in the former Plaszów camp September 5, 1946. Amon Göth – Unpublished Document by Robin O'Neil, The Camp Men – French MacLean, former Camp Plaszów website – www.cekie.krakow.pl/oboz_plaszow, USHMM, Holocaust Historical Society http://www.holocaustresearchproject.org/ghettos/krakow/amongoth.html

Göth's character was also featured in Spielberg's *Schindler's List* and Father mentions him in Chapter 14.

8

The Second Deportation
and the Deportation of Children

The second deportation started in September 1942 by means of dogs, convoy, and checks. We had to show our IDs. Each time I and my wife had to go outside and show our ID with the stamp of the swastika. The German soldiers asked the question: "Is someone hidden here?" I said, "Where would I hide someone? There is no hiding place."

"Otherwise you and your wife and your children will be shot."

They did not notice that there was a light blond child and one with very dark hair. They came in waves and went from house to house with dogs and took people without proper papers to a big place called *Umschlagplatz*. These people were doomed to die, by gas or to be shot. The deportation lasted about one week.[1]

There were about 200 people in both hiding places—there might have been up to 250 or 300 people. I did not keep count. It was a matter of minutes. There were about thirty people in the smaller hiding place, which was the one we had set up. There were about 170 to 200 people in the larger one, the one that was entered through the alcove.

On Friday, September 11, it was the day before the Jewish New Year, *Rosh Hashanah*, and the Germans came to every house, and all inhabitants who still remained had to go to the big square, to the *Umschlagplatz*. We watched as thousands of people under guard were being readied for death, to be sent to Auschwitz. And we stood and looked on. It was around eight o'clock in

---

1 The deportation took place September 10–15, 1942. It is unclear exactly when Dad led the people to their hiding place, but presumably several days before the start of the deportation.

the morning. The sun was burning, and we had not brought anything along. We had not eaten breakfast yet because they had come early, and everyone had to get out right away; without even a glass of water or an apple, without anything. There we stood. It was the start of an *Aktzie*.[2] The Germans dragged Jews out of numerous hiding places, which they had uncovered, and added them to the transport. And we just stood there together with the inhabitants of the house, including the two sisters who also had the *Hochheitssiegel*, and we prayed that we would not see anyone from our hiding place. And thank God, it was already evening, and not a single person from our hiding place was there, which meant that it had not been discovered. By now, we thought we would be going home since the Germans had already sent the people under guard, those without proper IDs, in the direction of the train station, to be transported off in wagons. The transports had already been dispatched. As I mentioned it was *Erev Rosh Hashanah*, the eve of the Jewish New Year. And there we still stood.

When it turned evening, we found out that there was an *Aktion* against children, despite their promises that every mother could keep one child. These gangsters, the Gestapo and soldiers, had erected a barrier and we had to run in a goose-step fashion. They formed two lines. We saw that young people, both men and single women, were directed to the right line and women with one or more children went to the left one and then had to sit down on the ground. It turned out to be an *Aktion* of children.[3]

There were about five thousand or six thousand or perhaps even ten thousand people or more in the *Umschlagplatz*. Then, that horrible moment approached. What should one do with the children? Should one go with the children or abandon them and save one's self? I have to tell you, *leider Gottes* (very unfortunately), the following: I was well known in town and had friends among young married couples and they would come to me to seek advice: "What is to be done?" As I already stressed earlier, I always acted according to logic. So, I would say: "Leave the children; let them lie. Why should we deliver more victims, mothers and children?" Everyone knew where that transport went; it went to the *Himmelkommando* (literal translation: commando to

---

2 Yiddish term describing the roundup of Jews; *Aktion* is the same term in German.
3 Since this was a children's *Aktion*, the mothers were probably to sit with the children for expediency. Later some mothers and fathers decided to be deported with their children.

heaven); it went to be gassed, it went to death. "Go and save yourselves, and if you survive you can have other children." It was horrible; it was the most horrible moment. And I also acted accordingly with our own child. I told my wife, "Let's run and leave the child." The child was two-and-a-half years old. So, we ran and left the child. We had to go through a checkpoint.[4] There were hundreds of people in front of us. We had to move in a running march. As our child saw us run, she started to run after us and started to scream and cry. She was not used to a situation in which her mother would leave her behind and run. We left our heart and soul with the child. We ran, but we turned around to see what was happening. And we saw this *Ordnungsdienst* (German for "guard") lift up the child and ask, "Whom does this child belong to?"[5] I stopped running; I went back and I told the guard, "Let go of the child; get away from the child," and I took the child in my arms and said to my wife, "You are not the mother of the child. Stay behind me." I came to the checkpoint with the child in my arms, and my wife was running after me. The guard asked, "Where is the mother of the child?" I said, "The mother was deported." At that moment, my wife came from behind and said, "I am the mother." The guard ordered me to go to the right and my wife to the left, where the mothers with children were. But I said, "No, I am going with them." At that moment even one of the criminals among them said to me, "Well, if you are stupid, then go with them."

And so I went. There were several others who went with their children. And I, I acted against my logic when I delivered not only the mother but also the father of the child. I went so to say voluntarily as he had told me to go to the right, the side to live, while the mother went with the child to the left. I said, "No, I am going with the child." He told me, "If you are so stupid, then go along," And so he put me to the side of death. That is the way the *Aktion* unfolded.

I need to tell you that my cousin Zigmund Grünkraut was hiding in our hiding place with his two daughters, Fedula and Siegrid, because he did not have the *Hochheitssiegel*, whereas his wife did. When I realized that each mother was allowed to keep one child if she had the *Hochheitssiegel*, I took the younger

---

4 Dad is crying.
5 We, Leon and Felicia, assume it was a German guard. Dad uses the terms militia, Jewish police, and *Ordnungsdienst* interchangeably.

child, Fedula, from the hiding place. Why should the child who was nine years old suffer when the mother was allowed to keep one child? I remember Fedula lay behind the bed whenever her parents went to work. There were sacks that were used to hide the child.[6] The child was nine years old. The child knew that the parents were working, her father in the East train station and her mother worked along with Fedula's older sister, Siegrid, in a clothing workshop. Siegrid was physically large and looked like a sixteen- year-old girl, though she was at most twelve or twelve and a half years old. She had a typical Aryan appearance, light blond hair with green eyes, and she was as beautiful as a porcelain figurine, the finest porcelain from Meissen. Before it got dark, Fedula crawled out of her hiding place and warmed up the stove and prepared dinner. She fixed noodles and other dishes, so that when her parents returned home, they could sit down at the table and be served dinner by Fedula. A nine-year-old girl!

After they took us to the *Umschlagplatz* and we realized that it was an *Aktion* for children, Fedula's mother came to me and said, "Listen, Schlomek, somebody has to look after Siegrid. You are going with the transport. Take Fedula and do what you can. I have to stay; if not, the people in the hiding places will perish from hunger and other causes."

After the *Aktion*, which lasted about two hours or longer, a large number of babies, some two months old, some six months old, some one year old, were left behind in the square of the *Umschlagplatz*. They were screaming. The guard chose some of the men selected to live, those who had the *Hochheitssiegel*, to place the children in baby carriages, like sardines, two or three per carriage. As there were no more trains going to Auschwitz, the children and adults were transported outside of town. They led us into an immense square, which was full of sand. In Polish, it was called *Piaskówka* (*piasek* means "sand" in Polish). There were giant military stables. The floors were lined with curled wood shavings, but there were no horses. There were five such giant stables. It was already night, the eve of *Rosh Hashanah*. My wife, our child, and I were in the first stable. Others were in the second and third stable. All were full with women and children.

---

6 It is unclear if the child was hiding in the sack or if the sack was used to hide or cover the child.

It was Friday, *Erev Rosh Hashanah*. During the night at the stables, there were loud screams from children who were without their mothers because the mothers had left them behind. The children were soiled and their behinds were full of feces and they were thirsty and hungry. It was like in a slaughterhouse. It was unimaginable. You heard nothing but the cries and screams of the children. And even if their mothers were present, small children of eight or ten months screamed because there was nothing to drink and nothing to eat, and they were hungry and thirsty. Around midnight, the Jewish militia came in and brought a big pot used to boil laundry, filled with soup.[7] But it was impossible to drink the soup because we had no cups and no utensils with which to eat. They had not brought any utensils. So I took my handkerchief and soaked my handkerchief in the big pot with the soup and let the screaming babies who were lying near me suck on it in order to quiet them down. People were eating the soup with their hands, as they had not eaten the whole day since eight o'clock in the morning. Most children had not even had any breakfast, and they were hungry. And that is how the soup was dispensed off. And then the militia left, and the doors were locked.

The first day of *Rosh Hashanah* arrived. At dawn, I saw two guards at the entrance with a rifle. I lay down next to the entrance and asked them for a cigarette. There was one German guard and a Polish policeman. I said to the policeman, "Here are 1,000 *złotys*; give me a cigarette," as I was a smoker. The policeman was a very fine young man and he said, "Very unfortunately I am not a smoker. I would gladly give you a cigarette for free but I have none. You are all such poor victims." You could see that he felt sorry for us. So I said to him through this opening on the bottom of the wall, "Maybe we could have some water," because we had stood the whole day with the sun burning like crazy, without anything to drink or eat. He said he would speak to the German soldier. So, they opened the gate, and I volunteered with two other people to get water. They had a giant bucket and we went to the well and dipped it into it and brought in water, once, twice.

We wanted to get water for the third time when we saw wagons packed with Jews, men and women, which were headed in our direction. Probably,

---

7 Laundry was "boiled" in large kettles before washing machines were available.

various hiding places had been discovered in the meantime by the Gestapo and the police. Several wagons were coming toward us to join us for the transport. They carried Orthodox Jews. They were bruised and bloody, without their hats. They had been beaten because they did not want to cut off their *peyes* and beards. When the soldier who was guarding us with the machine gun noticed the wagons, he said, "Quick, back inside," because he had acted on humanitarian grounds in order to help us. Soldiers, officers, even high-ranking officers from the army were afraid of the Gestapo. He therefore did not want to start up anything with the Gestapo and again locked us up in the stable.

Later that day (first day of *Rosh Hashanah*), the Gestapo and the chief of the employment agency and the commander of the *Ordnungsdienst* arrived and came to our stable first. There were perhaps six or seven Gestapo members, and they positioned themselves at the entrance. The man from the employment agency and other Gestapo members went to the middle of the stable. They had a list of names; the chief of the employment agency started to call out names. Though I stood fairly close to him, it was impossible to hear what he was yelling because the children were screaming. The three Gestapo members who were posted at the entrance took out their pistols and shot in the air to get some quiet. The children became scared and started crying even louder. The older people were tense, trying to find out what this was all about. We had no way of knowing what they wanted. Then, the commander of the security service called out that he had a loud voice and that he would do the reading. That he did. But it was the same problem; we heard nothing of what he was yelling out and what he was reading. I then approached him and said to the head of the employment agency, "Sir, I have a loud voice. Give the list to me. I am going to read." And I saw a list of names and I yelled out the names as loud as I could, along with the first names and the names of their wives and children if there were any. I read the first name three times, the second name also three times, the third name also three times, the fourth also three times. But nobody responded. Then I looked at the fifth name, and I saw my name, Lederberger, Salomon and Mrs. Tosia and daughter Felicia. When I read out my name, I said to the chief, "That's me, that's me." He said: "You go out then; go outside." I said to the chief, "I have two children." Though Fedula was blond, she was not very lightly blond. The Gestapo member butted in, "You go with your child and disappear." But Fedula held me by the jacket, and I led her by her little hand. It was a long stable, about a hundred and fifty to two hundred meters long and the Gestapo men were posted at the exit. I approached them and I took the child out literally in front of the eyes of the Gestapo. I stole the second child out with my daughter. A Gestapo man asked me, "Where are you going?" I said, "I was on the list, I and two children," He said, "Lie down." My wife got scared: "What did you do? What if they discover the truth?" I said, "In this confusion they surely won't notice Fedula. Be calm, calm yourself."

Afterward the Gestapo men went to the second stable. Nobody really knew what this was all about. Only later I found out why they took us out. Then another family was taken out. I also saw an acquaintance, Mr. Lessinger, come out of the third stable with his wife and his daughter Minka. He was a dentist, actually a dental technician. He was about two hundred or a hundred and fifty meters away from me. I saw him standing there talking to a Gestapo officer. Then, I heard the Gestapo man say, "You go back inside." He probably had asked to save his brother or his brother-in-law who also was in that stable. I don't know. He sent him back inside. All together, including children, we were forty-nine living souls. They put us in peasants' wagons and led us back into the ghetto.

The Gestapo was still present in the ghetto. The ghetto was in the final stages of liquidation, and those who had stayed behind were housed in a few buildings. Those who were able to work stayed there. There were a few hundred or a few thousand people left, I do not know. We saw Jews sitting on the ground as the Germans continued to search for hiding places in order to flush out Jews. Of course, those people who were discovered were shot to death. They were put on carts and the corpses were covered with their prayer shawls. Some of them were taken to the cemetery.

Later, we found out that everybody in the stables was deported from *Piaskówka* the following day. Apparently, empty trains had arrived. They transported them to Auschwitz. That is how we survived.

🗐 Historical Notes

Josef Mueller's testimony, continued. Here is the continuation of testimony by Josef Mueller, former commander of the SS Camps in Kraków, describing the second deportation in Tarnów:

> This *Aktion* could possibly have taken place a few days before Miechow … which I will now describe. This *Aktion* began, in the same manner as the others. [I was told] that I must escort Fellenz (another SS officer) again on this journey… We left Kraków and drove in an easterly direction. The journey ended … on the square in Tarnów… next to the Tarnów ghetto…. On the square I saw many SS-*Führer* and police officers… Further on the square, I saw many Jews… As I was waiting there … vehicles with Waffen-SS troops arrived … about 10–12 vehicles… The Jews were marched in groups of about 30, onto that square, from the houses … [and] were loaded into the vehicles and driven away. These vehicles returned after a while empty. Whenever there was no vehicle available on the square, the Jews were made to sit on that square. With the Jews, I am referring again to men, women, the old and the young. These … groups … were brought there by men of the SS Company and guarded by them… The events themselves are remembered by me very well. These I will never be able to forget, not in my whole lifetime… [When] it became lunch time, I felt hunger… I went to the German House [to eat]… Having drunk my beer, I left the German House. I saw there, that the Jews, in contrast to the morning, were now being driven off in vehicles as well as being marched off on foot, in groups of 30. The guard escort was in any case, carried out by the Waffen-SS men… As I had nothing to do, I went in that direction where the Jews were being taken to. I must add that the ghetto, or the part of the ghetto, from which the Jews were being driven out of, was surrounded by police units… I went… in that direction, to which the Jews were being taken to… I then came across a chapel… As

soon as I came near to that chapel I could hear shooting. They were single shots which were fired from several weapons. The firing was quite intense, but I could establish that they were single shots... I walked a while on the street which ran along the side of the wall [behind the chapel], which surrounded the cemetery. As I walked along that way, the firing became ever louder... I came at last to the cemetery entrance gate. The wall there was somewhat set back. As I came to that gate, a lorry came towards me, from the opposite direction. The lorry was fully loaded with Jews... At last I entered the cemetery, the lorry which I came across approaching from the opposite direction, stopped at the gate. The Jews were offloaded, as I came to that gate, the lorry just drove away on its return journey. I could however see that the driver of the lorry was a member of the Waffen-SS... The lorry came to a stop in such a position that the Jews could only go into the cemetery. On the cemetery entrance gate I noticed Kleinow... Kleinow was wearing the uniform of a SS-*Führer*. The rank insignia indicated that he was a SS-*Hauptsturmführer*. He was wearing uniform trousers and high boots... In his hand he was holding a pistol... From the Jews that were alighting from the above mentioned vehicles, some were hesitating. They did not want to enter into the cemetery. They have clearly noticed what was about to happen to them there. Kleinow grabbed the ones that were hesitating, by their chest, and killed them with his revolver, through a shot in the neck.

Immediately as I entered the cemetery I have noticed several bodies already lying there, in the immediate vicinity of Kleinow. There must have been some 8-10 bodies there. I have seen myself as Kleinow killed 2-3 Jews that arrived in those lorries, with shots into their necks.

I continued walking very slowly, further inwards. As the cemetery gate was cleared of the vehicle, I could look deep into the cemetery. I could see there barrels of lime, stacked against the wall next to the chapel. Further, I could see lying there, heaps of clothing. I could also see Jews running about, some of them had shovels in their hands. What they were doing with them, I have been unable to establish. Others were busy working at the heap of clothing... I cannot state how many Jews were killed on that day. They were however several hundred... It was not known to me that on the same day, Jews were also loaded onto a train on the railway station. On the journey back the liquidation of Jews has not been discussed...

Everything is written down as I have wished.

I confirm this report as correct with my signature.

Signed; J. Mueller

Holocaust Research Project, "Statement by Joseph Mueller, Former Commander of the SS Camps in Krakow," http://www.holocaustresearchproject. org/ghettos/jmueller.html.

9

Return to the Ghetto:
The Reason for Our Release

We came back to our house, the Michalewicz House, where the several hundred people were still in their hiding places. We went upstairs and were given soup. When I came back to our room, there was great joy. The inhabitants of the house opened the windows and shouted out loud, "Schlomek is here! Schlomek is here!"

What had really happened? Why had the Gestapo taken us out? The reason I was taken out of the transport by the Gestapo was that the vice president of the *Judenrat*, Mr. Józef Fast, had his mother and stepfather in my hiding place. By the way, the head of the Jewish Council's sister, his brother-in-law, and his two nephews were also in our hiding place. His name was Vogelman (the head of the Jewish Council). Whenever a Jewish family was deported, the Gestapo first thoroughly searched the whole apartment, took out valuables such as gold, silver, jewelry, fine rugs, and oil paintings, and then they sealed the apartment with a note: "This apartment is under the authority of the SD (*Sicherheitsdienst*, German for "security service"). Any attempt to enter is punishable by death." Since Józef Fast's mother was in our hiding place, he was afraid that if we were deported he would not be able to get her out. The Gestapo members who cleared out these houses was part of a team called Death. They would have surely discovered the hiding places during their search and everything would have blown up.

I then found out how I got on the list and the reason the Gestapo pulled out the people and me from the transport. It started to dawn on the Gestapo that they needed some Jews with certain skills, such as craftsmen and so forth.

In general every big-shot Gestapo officer had his personal Jewish *mosiek* (Yiddish for "gofer"), such as his personal shoemaker, his personal tailor, his personal watchmaker, his own silversmith, and other artisans who worked for him, without pay of course, except for an occasional piece of chocolate. The Gestapo, therefore, had work in progress. Let's say one had three dresses for his wife which were already cut up; another had three suits for himself; yet another a pair of officer's boots that were being made. The Gestapo received allowances for fabric and all the orders would be lost if these craftsmen were to be deported. This Gestapo man was looking for his shoemaker and that one for his watchmaker. And now in this whirlwind created by the deportation, these people were taken away. There was a great *tohu wawohu* (biblical Hebrew for "chaos"). Therefore, the Gestapo made up lists of the skilled craftsmen who had been deported or were to be deported, as they were at risk of losing them. The Gestapo found out from the director of the employment agency, which was located in a shack in the center of the *Umschlagplatz*, where these craftsmen had been sent. The head of the employment agency asked who knew how to type. Józef Fast, who had been director of Generalissimo, an Italian insurance company, knew how to type and volunteered. He realized that this was an opportunity to remove me and other people from being deported. The Gestapo men called out the names of their tailors, shoemakers, watchmakers, and so forth. It was then that Józef Fast asked if he could also name a very important person from the Jewish Council, though I was not a member. The Gestapo officer said, "OK, write that name down." So Fast wrote my and my wife's name in order to take us out, to save us and to save his mother as well as all the people who were in hiding. That, then, was the reason I was retrieved from the stable. Had I not gone along with my wife and child, no amount of money would have been enough to take my wife out. Thanks to the fact that I went with my wife and child, they also released my wife and my child, since I was the head of the family.

I then let all the people out of the hiding places. It was truly amazing; I was regarded higher than the Jewish God Himself. I was the only one they had to thank that they were saved. They were let out and left. Unfortunately, I have to admit a little mishap. I went upstairs to the hiding place at night with a lantern in order to retrieve some clothes and found all the suitcases empty. I guess they took all my belongings with them. But that is only a side issue, sort of beside the point. It was a matter of life or death. Ultimately, what did gold matter? Back in the stable a Jewish German girl had come to me and said, "I know you. You are the jeweler from Krakowska Street." She said she had jewelry with her and I should take it as she was afraid they would find it on her and beat her up. I told her, "Listen, you can just throw it away, because our lives are worthless and the jewelry is certainly worthless. We are all condemned to death." She showed it to me. Well, later I went to the guard who guarded us. I said to him, "Take it." I wanted to give it to him. There were gold chains, gold coins, and jewelry. He said, "What should I do with it? Throw it away?" The girl stood by us, so I told her, "Throw it away if you are afraid. I do not need it; I don't want it."

10

Mother and Felicia Escape from Tarnów

After things calmed down and all the dead were buried in the cemetery, I said to my wife, "Once in a lifetime you can hit a windfall like that, but never twice. Now, that's the end of this. Now we are going to get Aryan papers, and you must disappear with the child. I, as a single male, can do anything. I can join the underground. I can go into the forest. I can defend myself. I can jump out of a transport train." That was October 1942, I was thirty-three years old, and I was athletic. I could walk 60 kilometers a day; I could ride a bike for 150 kilometers; I could climb mountains; I knew how to ski. I was a strong and healthy man. So I told her I was going to arrange for Aryan papers. There was someone who did this for money. The underground organizations probably gave them out at no charge. I procured Aryan papers for my wife and for myself in the name of Ślusarczyk. Anna Zofia Ślusarczyk for my wife, Józef Ślusarczyk for myself, and Franciszka Felicja Ślusarczyk for our child. I got these papers through a contact person, who was actually a distant relative of my wife's. His name was Naschek Keller, an engineer. He had contacts with the underground organization and he got the papers 100 percent at no cost.

The underground organization arranged these false papers or documents and identification cards. Shame on him for making money on that. He charged quite a bit. In other words, he traded with Jews. He is still alive and lives in Vienna, Austria (as of 1981). He is a manufacturer and a textile engineer. For us Jews it is shameful. Later, I will tell you how I acquired papers for people when I was in Warsaw living on Aryan papers. I made contact with the underground organization and procured papers for people. There were liaisons to the underground organization who were Poles. There were several of them. One of them was Janek, who later on was accused of having blackmailed Jews. I do not know if it was confirmed. Then there was Janka, a woman, and there was a man from Kraków, a *Volksdeutsche* (ethnic German). Another liaison was Julek Steiger, whom I had sent to Tarnów, and his son, Rysiek Steiger. There was also Julek Merz. But this is for later and is not relevant right now.

As I emphasized before, I said to my wife that once in life you can hit a jackpot and that we had hit that jackpot when they took us out of the transport, because the entire transport went to Auschwitz and nobody survived. The whole transport was killed. So I got the papers in the name of Ślusarczyk, Józef for myself and for my wife Ślusarczykowa because in Polish the feminine ends in "owa."[1] I searched out a contact with an engineer who was a customer of mine, Mr. Asdu. He had a PhD in chemistry and was an engineer of forestry, taking care of forests. He gave me a letter of recommendation to his colleague, also an engineer of forestry, who lived in a resort town called Iwonicz Zdrój. And then I said to my wife, "Pack what you absolutely need and drive to the resort town. I arranged for it." My wife said, "Absolutely not"; that she would stay here and she would die together with me. I said, "No, you will go, because I want to live together with you." She did not want to budge. So I brought a suitcase and randomly took things out of the closet; linen and underwear, whether it was necessary or not. There was a tremendous commotion. I was very upset, very aggravated, and of course, my wife was as well, because she was to go out all alone as an Aryan to a foreign place among strangers and play the role of a Pole and a Christian. That was a tremendous adjustment.[2]

After the second deportation, I worked for *Höheres Fahrkraftamt*, HKP. It was a garage that repaired cars for the military and SS. I was assigned to the garage as an expert mechanic. Of course, I had no clue how to be a mechanic. I hardly worked at all. I got placed there through a connection with a previous neighbor of mine by the name of Kudelski, who was a close friend of Mr. Dagnan, the owner of the garage and a *Volksdeutsche*. I asked Kudelski to help me

---

1 Felicia has both Mother's and Father's identification cards.
2 Mother was able to "blend in" in the Polish environment because of "good" appearance despite her black hair; she had a "non-Jewish" nose and did not wear glasses.

get the job, which he managed to do so. The master mechanic of the garage was a man by the name of Skorupka. His son was a chauffeur. He used to borrow the car from Dagnan.[3]

I led my wife and the child, I must say by force, to this garage. And so Skorupka's son drove my wife and the child to Iwonicz Zdrój with the letter of recommendation from the engineer Asdu. The letter said that my wife was with her child and that her husband was a Polish officer who had gone underground, that the Gestapo was giving her trouble and always wanted to know where her husband was. Therefore, she had to leave town in order to get rid of the harassment by the Gestapo. That then was the pretext for her trip. My wife went to the engineer, of course, without the Jewish star armband, which she had taken off, as she already had the Aryan papers.

As I said before, as a young athletic man, I could always manage and never give up. But when you are responsible for your wife and child you are duty bound to be with them through all the dangers, and your movements are much more restricted. As a single man I could jump from wherever was necessary or run away from anywhere or forcefully resist. Alone, I was free to act. And my wife and child indeed arrived to the resort town, and the engineer met her and found her a room. The room was sublet by a woman, Mrs. Richter. Around Christmastime the woman became suspicious that my wife was Jewish.

One day, my wife came home. She had left the child at home because it was a harsh winter. She went to buy something and when she came home, Mrs. Richter said to her that she wanted more money for the rent. My wife asked her why. The woman said, "I know already everything from your daughter. Don't play games with me. If you are going to play games with me, I will report you." I was happy that she had found a good place. I did not know the circumstances yet. One day, I received a letter through a messenger, as there was no mail in the ghetto, neither incoming nor outgoing. This man was a man to be trusted, and she sent a letter with him. It was a terrible letter. She wrote that she wanted to go back to the ghetto and if I did not send someone to bring her back to the

---

3   In answer to a question by the interviewer, Dad says that he worked there as a Jew wearing the yellow armband. Dad also notes that initially there were about forty people working at the garage and then later they cut it down to ten.

ghetto, then she had no other way out but to go to the police and turn herself in and announce that she was Jewish and end it all. She claimed she could not go on under these circumstances, as the landlady suspected that she was Jewish, and she stole various things from her. In response to that letter I asked around. I had a friend, Haskel Hollender, whom I mentioned earlier. His son Zigmund Hollender was an engineer, though I do not know what kind of engineer. The son referred me to a certain man by the name of Janek (the liaison to the underground mentioned earlier). I sent him to Iwonicz so he could bring her back. But Zigmund Hollender advised me she should be brought to Milanówek, because there lived a family by the name of Szpilman whom I had saved in my hiding place—Abraham Szpilman, his wife and two sons, and his daughter-in-law with a grandchild. Milanówek is 363 kilometers north from Iwonicz near Warsaw, where my wife stayed. It was a nice little town with small houses where people from the big cities went to relax, like a resort. So my wife went to the Szpilmans' in Milanówek.[4]

All this took place about two or three weeks after the second deportation, when I was able to get the papers. I also arranged papers for relatives of mine, the family Grünkraut. They had stayed with us when we were still living on the main street in Tarnów. They were from Germany, from Duisburg, Germany, I think. They had come to Poland, to Bielsko-Biała, which is an industrial town that produced textiles. There they settled. He had managed to smuggle a certain amount of gold dollars with the help of a diplomatic messenger, which he then converted into cash. That was still before the war. He worked there when the Germans invaded Poland. The Germans right away incorporated those border towns into the Reich (as Germany was called at the time), so that all Jews fled from there. So did he with his wife and two daughters. Siegrid was about eleven years old and Fedula about nine. Siegrid was ash blond and Fedula was also blond, but darker. They came to Tarnów and could not find a place to live. I

---

4 When Mother arrived at Mr. Szpilman's, he told her, "You have come just in time, Tosia. Two hours ago I had a visit from the *Granatowe* ["the navy ones," a nickname for the Polish police due to the color of their uniforms]. I have to abandon the apartment, and I have to get out, to move on." Mother did not know what to do as she had traveled all night from Iwonicz to Milanówek with a small child. She thought of turning herself in to the Gestapo, but Szpilman told her, "No, don't go to the Gestapo. We'll figure something out."

had quite a big apartment, a four-room apartment, and I said they could live with me. Of course I did not profit from it; I did not charge rent. They lived quite a while with us until we had to leave when all Jews had to evacuate the main street. As I said earlier, I managed to get a house with a garden and they moved to an apartment somewhere outside of town. Later, when all Jews had to be in the ghetto, Mr. Grünkraut worked at the East train terminal. He worked very hard. He had to march four to five kilometers to his workplace at the train station at four o'clock in the morning and would come home quite late. He and his oldest daughter, Siegrid, were in my hiding place. As mentioned earlier, I had snuck out Fedula in front of the Gestapo and brought her back to her parents during the second deportation.

So, we lived in the Michalewicz House until after the second deportation, which took place in September of 1942 and which lasted about one week. In October, I sent my wife and child away. At that time we believed that nothing would happen to people who had work, because the Germans needed workers. I had a job with the HKP working in the garage. I went to work in the morning and returned every evening to the ghetto. In 1942, I was thirty-three years old, having been born in 1909.

But then in a fairly short period of perhaps two to three months after the second deportation, the third deportation took place. There were rumors that it was about to happen.

The Sisters

The two sisters who lived in the Michalewicz House and who worked in a garment factory, asked me if I could help them get to Warsaw, as they were afraid to travel alone (that was after the second deportation). They supposedly had an apartment in Warsaw. The owner of the garage of the HKP was a sergeant in the German military. He had a car. Generally cars, horses, and even other vehicles had all been confiscated by the Germans, and there was no way for a Pole to get one. The two sisters asked me to ask the boss to bring them to Warsaw with his car. They wanted me to arrange that and they were ready to pay him for this with a diamond ring. It was a little bit dangerous because I was not so friendly with him. He knew me by sight but had no contact with me. However, when it was a matter of rescuing two Jewish girls, I took the risk. I approached him and told him I had urgent business to discuss. He took me into his office and asked, "What is this all about? What do you want?" They usually addressed Jews with the informal *Du* (you). So I said, "I have two Christian acquaintances and they would like to go to Warsaw for Christmas to spend with their family. Would you be willing to take them in exchange for a nice present?" As it happened he was from Hamburg and was to go to Hamburg for Christmas vacation. So I told him he could bring his wife a diamond ring as a gift for Christmas. The first question he asked me was if the Christian ladies had a "good appearance" (meaning they did not look Jewish). I told him, "For God's sakes, you don't believe that these are Jewish ladies?" He answered, "I believe everything, but I want to know if they have a good appearance." I said, "perfect," as they really had no resemblance to Jewesses, I mean stereotypically. So he agreed.

However, in the meantime a mishap occurred. He drove somewhere out of town and his car was wrecked. He got out of it intact, but told me that unfortunately it would not work out, because there were several spare parts that were missing and that he himself had to take the train. I informed the sisters. The sisters then came to me with another suggestion. I was closely befriended with Haskel Hollender, though I was thirty-three years of age and he was perhaps thirty years older than I. His son Zigmund was my friend as well. Haskel Hollender was a very good friend and I had helped him a lot when he came back home from Lemberg,[1] which was Russian-occupied territory. He had no money, though he used to be one of the wealthiest men; he owned forests, houses, and factories, all of which had been confiscated. They confiscated his house, and he had to go to the ghetto. Haskel Hollender worked at the East train terminal. He was an elderly person over age sixty but healthy, and he marched to work. He had contacts with railroad employees. The younger sister was the girlfriend and the mistress of Józef Fast, the vice president of the Jewish Council.

So, the girls came to me and told me that they could not approach Hollender because he was mad at them since Józef Fast was either a nephew or a close relative of Haskel Hollender. Haskel Hollender was angry at the girls because Jósef Fast was unfaithful to his wife. The sisters asked me to tell Hollender, without disclosing their names, that two girls wanted to get out of town and that he should arrange for the train trip. And indeed he arranged the train ride. Hollender owed me a debt, because during the second deportation his wife and a nephew were hiding in my hiding place. Hollender sent two railroaders to my garage claiming that they could be trusted. I asked them if they were prepared to accompany the two young women to Warsaw. I told them that the sisters had a girlfriend in Warsaw who had arranged an apartment for them. The sisters had forged identification cards with Polish names. The railroaders agreed to do so in exchange for a certain sum, which I don't remember, since that was of no

---

1 Also known as "Lwów" or "Lvov"; now it is Lviv in the Ukraine.

importance. So I informed the sisters that the railroaders were prepared to get them to Warsaw. Then one sister came up with another matter. "You are aware that it is winter now and we had to hand in our fur coats and collars to the Germans. Two elegant ladies like us cannot ride in the train in winter without fur coats and not arouse suspicion." It was winter in Poland and every woman, even a peasant's daughter and certainly two elegant ladies like they were, had a fur coat. They requested that I acquire fur coats for them. I responded, "Where from do you think I can get fur coats in Poland? In the ghetto, one cannot find this."

"Yes, but you travel outside the ghetto," she said, and by the way, "Regina, the wife of Jósef Fast, the vice president of the Jewish Council, has given her silver-fox fur coat to the vice president of Generalissimo to hide, since she did not want to turn it over to the Germans." Fast had handed it over to the insurance company's vice president. Józef Fast probably told his mistress, the younger of the two sisters, that his wife had a fur coat and where it was located, after she told him of her problem. And I, Schlomek, as I was called, should talk to Regina, who would probably sell the fur coat. So, a new situation arose. I approached Regina and told her that my wife was on Aryan papers, which was a lie. Only in an emergency do I say a lie, but it was a matter of life and death for two pretty girls. The older sister was a virtuoso pianist with the BBC after the war and gave concerts before the war. I told Regina that my wife was in Warsaw and that she had no fur coat, since I had burned them all at night—my wife's, my father's, and my mother's. I burned them in an oven by pouring alcohol and benzene over the coats. I did that because I did not want to deliver the fur coats to the Germans, though it was under the penalty of death. I burned them in the cellar of my cousin, who had a house next to the house I lived in. We used a device used to boil clothes.[2] My cousin and I worked very hard, as leather burns only with difficulty. But we managed to do it, though it took all night.

Anyway, I talked to Regina. I said: "Listen, Regina, I heard from your husband that you have a fur coat, and my wife has difficulties going out of the house in Warsaw without a fur coat. I want you to sell me your fur coat."

---

2 Presumably a large steel kettle in which clothes were boiled to wash them thoroughly in those days before washing machines.

She spontaneously responded: "Please, I give it to you for free." I answered, "Regina, I do not want any gifts." She did not know, however, what the fur coat was worth and neither did I. I had a suggestion. During wartimes, consignment businesses had been established that dealt with used clothing, watches, furniture, and so on, since there were no normal deliveries of such goods. Many such businesses were privately owned. So Regina would inquire how much she would be offered for the coat, say five thousand or six thousand *złotys* more or less. Initially she balked; she did not want to accept money. I, however, had no interest in accepting any gifts from her. She finally gave me a note with the address, which I gave to one of the railroaders, asking him to fetch the fur coat. And so he did.

I then inquired from some Christian young men who worked in the consignment store, if they had any fur coats to sell, since it was a pity to use Regina's coat, which was a fox-fur coat with all accessories, including snout and tail, such as was worn in those days. I bought a Persian fur coat, a kimono, from him. He gave me the price and I bought it. And I hid it among wooden panels that he sold me as well.[3] The day came when I wanted to lead the two girls out of the ghetto. Our group did not have any guards, only a group leader, who was responsible for the group. The entrance to the ghetto was only about six hundred or seven hundred meters away from the garage and was on the same street. So I approached the group leader and said, "Listen, you have to do me a favor." We used to leave the ghetto at seven in the morning. "There are two girls who want to leave town, and I want to include them in our group." He said that was out of the question, that he would not risk his head. If the girls were caught, the group leader would be responsible. The two girls were already all prepared and waited to be led out of the ghetto. So I told the group leader: "You know what, stay home. Get yourself a sick note, and I will be the group leader, the substitute group leader." The other people from the group were also scared, but I said, "People, it's about saving two Jewish girls," and they agreed. So I became the group leader, and I led the group through the gate of the ghetto.

---

3 Dad presumably bought the second coat so that both sisters would have a fur coat for the train ride. It was of utmost importance for Jews living as Aryans to have everything to blend in the general population.

Everything was in order and I led them to the garage of Skorupka where there was a hut-like structure. From there I took out the fur coats, and the sisters adorned their coats with collars. Then the two railroaders arrived. They already had the suitcases for the two girls. They accompanied them to the train.[4] Before the girls left, I gave them one condition: I gave them the address of my wife, who lived in Milanówek and told them that upon arrival to deliver this fox-collar coat to my wife. My wife should find out what the coat was worth, because I had to pay for it. Indeed, they got out all right and arrived happily. They moved into a room, which their girlfriend had arranged for them. They then traveled to my wife and delivered the fox-fur. My wife sold it and I paid Regina.

---

4 It is unclear if the young men rode with them in the train.

 # Betrayal and the Third Deportation (November 1942)

One day the Gestapo issued a new ordinance that each business had to have a sign made out of sheet metal with a letter written on it. Every business had its own specific letter. Again another calamity befell us when 75 percent of members of our group who worked in the garage were deported. Only ten of us remained. Those ten workers received a special identification card with the letter Z. The secretary received ten IDs for those of us working in the garage for HKP. She called out various names; first this man, then others, and gave them their IDs. Names were called out for individuals, who came forth with the sheet-metal sign Z. The second, the third, the fourth, the fifth, the sixth, the seventh, the eighth, and the ninth name was called. I was not called. I wondered why, went to the secretary, and asked, "Why did everybody receive their ID except for me?" "Ask the boss," she answered. "What do you mean by ask the boss?" The boss was rarely present; he was on the go, coming and going, and I could not talk to him. Meanwhile, someone whispered into my ear that the boss had sold my number for a diamond ring to someone by the name of Unger. That was a violation of orders and regulations. I could not believe that such a thing was possible. In the meantime I walked illegally with my group who all had their IDs. I hid in the back of the group and hoped to catch Janek Dagnan, the boss. And finally, several days later, I succeeded to grab him, and I said, "Mr. Dagnan, where is my ID? You received an allocation for ten people, and I among them. Where is mine?" He answered that he received only nine. What a swindler and wheeler-dealer he was, claiming he only had received nine IDs. "But you received an allocation for ten and I am the tenth. Why did I not receive it?" So he tried to console me that he would go to the Gestapo and take care of it. In the meantime, Mr. Unger, whose name was placed instead of mine, interceded. And it turned out that it was indeed true what had been whispered to me in such a casual manner. So it looked like I was being excluded and those who had no work would be shot to death. Meanwhile, I continued to go illegally with the group.

One day while I was with the group, a Christian boy who worked there said to me, "Hide yourself because the entire ghetto is surrounded, and there is a deportation." So I hid somewhere in the area; I do not remember exactly where, as the area was very large. I hid between wooden boards and stayed there the entire day and night until the group returned the next day. I found out that there had been a deportation, that they had taken people out of the ghetto, and that they had taken whole groups of people who were at their workplaces. They cleaned out the ghetto, taking out several hundred or thousand people. I was not present, so I don't know exactly how many. The next day, as the group arrived, I was curious as to what happened. Luckily, I was told, they had not come into our garage. It might not have been worth their while to get only ten Jews, or maybe Dagnan had some useful connections. But they dragged out whole groups of other workers, numbering one hundred to three hundred, and deported them. The next day I went back to the ghetto with the group. I realized that I was in a tough situation. I was without a job, and at any moment, if they caught me, I would be finished. So I ran to the Jewish Council, where I had a friend, namely Mr. Fast. And I told him the story how Dagnan had betrayed me and that I was left to be shot, to be annihilated. And my friend, the vice president of the Jewish Council, told me, "We can hire you here in the Jewish Council."

"That is out of the question," I said. He wanted to hire me as a militia, the Jewish police force. The Jewish police conducted themselves very poorly as they helped to carry out orders of the Gestapo. They were known to even deliver their own siblings and parents. They took orders from the chief of police, who had to fill a certain quota of people who had to be delivered for deportation. "I am not suitable for this and it won't happen," I said. I could only help people and certainly not deliver them to their death. He told me, "If you do not want this position, though we think it is the safest, I know of a business run by Jósef Balzer, a commissioner (high rank in the militia) of a Jewish business. They deliver horse hair and pig hair, which is cleaned for usage in airplane seats for military use." Józef Balzer had requested from the Gestapo to assign him one hundred additional workers. Mr. Fast told me to wait for a while, and if the request was granted, he could accommodate me there.

I moved about in the ghetto since they were not looking for me there yet. It was dangerous to go with the group, which had an assignment of ten people and therefore could not have eleven. The group leader had already told me several times that he could not allow me, nor take it upon himself for me to join the group. So, I had no choice but to remain in the ghetto. And indeed they allocated Balzer fifty to a hundred people. I don't think it was one hundred, but at least fifty people. To be placed there every person had to pay the rather large sum of twenty thousand *złotys*. That was quite a lot. Jósef Balzer had his own *mosiek*, and Balzer pocketed all that money. Perhaps he gave some of it to his *mosiek*. The Jewish Council received an allocation of five or ten places for its own people. So Mr. Fast called me and informed me that I now was part of Balzer's workshop. "But you have to come up with twenty thousand *złotys*." I was pleased and agreed. So from then on I went outside the ghetto to the workshop, which was quite far from the city. The factory had belonged to a Jewish firm by the name of Hornig or something like that. They were known *Hassidim* (a branch of Orthodox Judaism emphasizing piety). They were learned and very pious. When the commissioner was not around, they prayed, laid *tefillin* (phylacteries), and studied the Torah. Early every morning, I went there with a transport, which was guarded by two armed men, and returned to the ghetto each evening.

As an aside, at Balzer's firm, I was known as the "protégé child" of the Jewish Council. The reason for that was I had not paid Balzer or his *mosiek*, who was his right hand. So because I did not deliver the money, people thought that the *Judenrat* had placed me with Balzer free of charge.[1]

---

1 Dad received one of the allocations given by the Jewish Council and paid the Jewish Council—not Balzer.

🗐 Historical Notes

Tarnów ghetto, October/November 1942. In his unpublished research on the ghettos of Galicia, and posted on www.holocaustresearchproject.org, Robin O'Neil describes events in the Tarnów ghetto in the fall of 1942.

> In October 1942 the ghetto was divided into two parts. Section A was organized as a forced labor camp with separate quarters for men and women … and it housed Jewish men, women and children aged over 12 years, all of whom were organized into working squads. … Section B held all Jews who did not work and Jewish laborers with large families. …
>
> On 15 November 1942 another *Aktion* took place in Tarnów… A significant number of Ghetto B inhabitants decided to hide in shelters, basements and other places to avoid detection. The Ghetto A Jews left for work. The Ghetto B Jews were ordered to report to the Magdeburger Platz, where they were made to surrender all valuables. They were ordered to kneel down while Gestapo officers … checked their documents in a brutal fashion. … At about midday the selected 2,500 Jews at the square were lined up in columns and marched under guard to the station, where they were loaded into goods wagons which were then closed and sealed with lead. The train left Tarnów station at about 6 p.m.

Holocaust Research Project, "Tarnow Ghetto," http://www.holocaustresearch-project.org/ghettos/tarnow.html.

Father's betrayal. In this chapter Father describes how his job placement in the Dagnan garage was taken by a Mr. Unger, who bribed the person in charge to receive this most precious and life-saving spot. Felicia got in touch with Dr. Israel Unger, the son of this Mr. Unger, through a search of Tarnów people on the website www.allgenerations.com. Dr. Unger confirmed that he, his parents, and his brother survived hidden in the Dagnan mill, and he remembers that his father gave Mr. Dagnan "some jewelry." Dr. Unger in turn, forwarded Felicia the following e-mail which he received from Adam Bartosz, curator of the

Regional Museum in Tarnów and which is available on the museum's website, www.muzeum.tarnow.pl. It is translated by Dorota Głowacka. Here are some pertinent excerpts from that e-mail:

> Hiding a person or a family carried not only a personal risk (denunciations on the part of one's neighbors, German searches), but it also required expensive maneuvers, such as preparing a relatively comfortable hideout with access to toilets, and be safe from potential informers. It is important to remember that the discovery of a hideout meant certain death to the owners of the apartment. Another difficulty was finding food, which was severely limited by the Germans. This is why the cases of hiding Jews in one's own home were rare and required immense heroism. We know very little about such cases, since even those who helped the Jews survive preferred to keep silent about it after the war, faced with the hostility on the part of the Christian inhabitants of Tarnów toward the Jews and toward those who had been helping them.
>
> This is why the discovery of a hideout in which a group of Jews survived the war, merits documentation. The hideout was located in the buildings of the Dagnan mill, which was demolished in 2001. The Dagnans built and managed a mill, a large workshop that produced parts for the mill machinery, repair shops, garages, and modern offices and services complex. The buildings of the mill became a hideout for a group of Jews, who stayed there for over a year.

Mr. Bartosz was told the story of the nine Jews by Mrs. Zofia Dagnan in February 2001 when the mill and the adjacent building were being torn down. That is when the hideout was discovered.

 **The Weapon**

I want to tell you an important and remarkable incident that happened before the liquidation of the ghetto, when I worked for Józef Balzer. The workshop was a wooden shed. The place was under supervision by the *Ordnungsdienst*, who had the key.

When somebody rang the doorbell, the guard opened the door. My work consisted of bundling up cut hair, which was put into sacks. Periodically, a truck would come by, and we would load up those sacks, which weighed sixty to eighty kilos, onto the truck. The first time I was told to lift those sacks I almost passed out, as I was not used to such heavy work. But I had to do it, and as time went on I was able to carry them. They felt like sacks of cement. I carried them from the second floor, where the horse and pig hair was cleaned, and loaded them on the truck. One day, I was working on the second floor when the bell rang. The door opened and a plumber, who worked with water and gas pipes, came in. He had been an academician and a colleague of a very good friend of mine. His name was Hebka. I forget his first name. When he came in, he was stunned to see me. He had been introduced to me when we still lived outside the ghetto. He was called in because something had to be fixed in the toilet. He called me over and asked me, "What are you doing here? Don't you know that the organization 'Death' dug out a long grave outside the city and that they unloaded lime and that this is prepared for you Jews?" I asked him, "What should I do? I have nothing. I cannot run away. Without a weapon I cannot go anywhere." "Run away! Anywhere," he said. "I will not go without a weapon because any stable boy can stab me to death, rob me, and deliver me to the Gestapo. I need a weapon." He said: "If you can get me three rolls of English cloth, I'll get you a weapon. I can even get you ammunition. I belong to an underground organization."

So it was agreed, and I promised him what he wanted. There were many rolls of cloth left over from people who had been deported. Often, these fabrics were sealed up in walls in cellars. People had constructed additional walls and hidden the goods in between. Whenever people were deported, there were Jews who knew where to look for the goods.[1] They would bang on walls and wherever there was a suspicion of a double wall they would tear it down. They especially searched in places of former clothing manufacturers and retailers. Tarnów used to be a big center of textile manufacturing.

The *Judenrat* had a militia under its jurisdiction. The militia was often tipped off by traitors who knew where fabrics were being hidden. Those traitors were Jews who ganged up on and beat the *Schaflers* until they divulged the location of the cloth. The *Judenrat* then warehoused the fabrics, claiming they needed them because of requisitions for fabric by the Gestapo. A neighbor of mine, Schy Stup, was in the higher echelon of the *Judenrat*, just below the director. I went to him because I knew that he was in charge of the fabric. I told him, "Schy, I need three rolls of fabric, two of them English cloth and one for riding pants," which required a special fabric, the name of which I don't remember anymore. He told me that he would sell it to me and how much it would cost. He wondered, however, how I would get it out of the ghetto. I told him that I needed it urgently for somebody, and that would be my problem. So I bought it from him and paid for it, of course, for cutthroat prices. I wrapped the fabric underneath my shirt when we marched to Józef Balzer's workplace. I had everything ready. Hebka had told me he would come at the end of the week.

At the end of the week, he came and asked me if I had the fabric. I said yes. "Did you bring the Browning?" I asked. He claimed that he was in touch with the underground organization and that he was supposed to get the weapon that day. Later, he was told it would not be until the next day. He assured me

---

1   Dad called them *Schaflers*. This was a slang term for thieves and looters of abandoned property. In Polish they are called *szabrownicy*.

that he would bring it then. I gave him the cloth on the promise that he would bring the Browning with the ammunition the following day. I trusted him, as he was a Communist and I regarded him as an idealist. A friend, also an academician, an engineer, had told me that I could trust Hebka and that he was an upright and fine human being. I had told Hebka that my wife lived on Aryan papers with a child in Warsaw and that I had stayed behind and wanted to go somewhere underground but could not do so without a weapon. I told him things that could cost me my head, but I trusted the man. The next day when he was supposed to bring me the weapon, I waited for him the whole day. In the evening we had to go back to the ghetto. A second, third, and fourth day went by and there was no sign of him. A week went by, and I did not see him or hear from him. There was a Christian boy who was twelve years old. His father had been the plumber of the high school, but since all schools were closed, as teaching and studying were forbidden, he had set up his plumbing workshop at Balzer's place. I took a piece of paper and wrote a note, which said: "Sir, I have been waiting for a long time; you promised me to deliver the goods on a certain day, at most one day later. I ask you to immediately take care of this matter. But should you not be able to deliver, I ask you to return the cloth, because that is all I own. You know my situation." I gave the boy the note to bring it to him. The boy came back with the assurance that Hebka would come tomorrow or at the latest the day after. The next day, as well as several more days, went by and nothing happened. So I called the boy again, explained to him where Hebka was, namely in the *Realgymnasium* (high school), and wrote again: "Listen, I see that you want to enrich yourself, but if you don't return my cloths or at least pay for them, I will come to you with my commissioner to get them." There were actually three commissioners, Jósef Balzer being the chief. He was in charge of our factory. The boy came back with the promise that he would come next day and would bring me the Browning. But again the same thing happened, and I realized that it was a flop.

Several days after I made the threat, somebody rang the bell, and the security guard opened the door. I worked upstairs, and we all looked to see who it might be—perhaps a Gestapo officer to apprehend somebody, or maybe just somebody who came to visit someone. I saw boots, officer's boots. The man was a stranger to me, who looked like a police agent or someone similar to that. He said something to the security guard, who then came inside the house and called me: "Lederberger, you are wanted." For a Jew to just have contact with a gentile meant the death penalty, both for the Jew and for the gentile. But my heart told me that something was not right, because I saw the German for the first time, and yet he was looking for me. So I thought right away that it had to do with Hebka. Jósef Balzer's *mosiek*, who by the way was a very Orthodox Jew, started yelling: "You are going to bring tragedy upon us with your gold dealings." He was very upset, but that did not faze me. I went downstairs and went to the German and said to him, "I am Lederberger. What do you want from me?"

He said, "Listen to me; I was at the police station. They arrested a man by the name of Hebka and they found three rolls of fabric at his place. During interrogations he admitted that he got them from a man called Lederberger who works at Jósef Balzer's place." Right away, I smelled a blackmail attempt. He wanted to get money out of me, so he sent a colleague. I said, "I thank you, but I have nothing to do with it and in God's name get out of here, get out!" and I led him to the door. I said to the security guard: "Open the door and let him out." The whole house observed the scene. I was agitated. The German said, "Hebka even said that your wife and child are living on Aryan papers in Warsaw." When he said that I realized that I was a lost man and I yelled, "Out!" and I gave him a kick in the ass. Now my whole body was shaking. What trouble did I get myself in? The *mosiek* came running to me and yelled that I should get out of the building, that I would bring disaster upon everybody, and that our Gestapo would come. I should get lost immediately. Everybody had seen how I had given him a kick in the ass and thought the man looked like a police agent or a secret agent. The *mosiek* said he would notify Richter, the other commissioner, to lead me back to the ghetto, as each commissioner had the right to lead Jews wearing a star in and out of the ghetto. About a half hour later, Erik Richter, the commissioner, arrived. He was a thin and tall man. The *mosiek* told him to bring me to the ghetto. I was glad, as I realized I was walking on burning coal, a large flame under my feet (literal translation), which could blow up at any time. Richter was also glad to see me leave and led me to the ghetto. I went to my friend Kuba Hier, who was a very respected member of the Jewish Council. I met him in the *Umschlagplatz*, the large square. We got along very well. I told Kuba what had happened. He answered: "Don't talk now; a bigger tragedy happened here. The Germans took two security guards—two brothers by the name of Stern—led them to the Jewish cemetery, and they were both shot to death. In the ghetto it is like *Tisha Be Av*.[2] Everybody is very depressed."

I told him: "Now you have to help me. You are friends with a plumber who works for the Gestapo, a Jew by the name of Biegeleisen or similar to that." I said, "I want to know one thing. Ask your friend Biegeleisen to go to his co-worker, Hebka, and tell him that as a colleague, he needs some kind of a gadget for the Gestapo." This was a pretext to see if Hebka really was under arrest and in jail as I was told by that man or whether he was at his regular job as usual. Biegeleisen had free entry to the workshop; he could come and go without a guard, though he always had to wear the Jewish star. We waited anxiously. He came back about an hour later and reported that he talked to Hebka, who gave Biegeleisen what he asked for and seemed absolutely calm. That news calmed me in that I was not in immediate danger. I figured logically that it would not be in Hebka's interest to turn me in to the Gestapo, since he would have to give up the three rolls of fabric. Besides, he could be punished to have dealt with a Jew. That's what my logic told me. This way I spent my time, until the final liquidation of the ghetto. The final liquidation occurred in September of 1943; I ran off in October.

---

2 *Tisha Be Av* refers to the ninth day of the Jewish month of Av, a Jewish day of mourning.

 # Amon Göth: The Final Liquidation of the Tarnów Ghetto

In September 1943, along came a certain Mr. Göth from Kraków, a man approximately two meters tall and broad-shouldered. Since it was night, most Jews were locked in the ghetto, which was surrounded by the Germans. During nights it was common in the ghetto to drink vodka heavily, so as to numb ourselves. It was also common to have sexual relationships. There were many married women without husbands and men without their wives and children, so that life was pretty loose, as everyone was virtually sentenced to death. I myself drank heavily almost every evening, and like a man sentenced to death, nothing mattered anymore. Money was of no concern as we were all sentenced to death. One night, we were suddenly awakened by the noise of people running in the ghetto. The ghetto was surrounded. The liquidation of the ghetto was happening. The next day these bandits entered the ghetto—the gendarmerie, the SS, the Gestapo, and the Polish police. It was ordered that members of every business had to come forth in the *Umschlagplatz*. Chaos and wailing ensued. Then Göth, who was the leader of the entire deportation, appeared. I did not stand too far from him. He shouted: "Quiet, quiet, please," and everybody became quiet. There were no more children around; the ghetto was already *Kinderrein* (cleansed of children). They had even dragged children out of the orphanages. Most children had already been deported during the second deportation. A special orphanage was established for the children who still remained. My friend Mr. Kuba Hier, who had been the director of a savings and loan institution in the neighboring town of Kraków, was the head of the orphanage. There may have been thirty or forty children in the orphanage. I don't know, as I was never there.

As I mentioned, in the *Umschlagplatz* businesses had to display their signs, such as "Józef Balzer, East Railroad Station," and so forth. We had to stand in a row behind the signs wherever we were working. I, of course, placed myself behind Józef Balzer's sign because I worked there. And Göth said, "Silence, silence; nobody is going to be harmed; you all will come with me to Płaszów where you will work and nobody is going to get hurt.[1] Every man and woman can take along twenty-five kilogram of baggage, such as clothing, underwear, and blankets." The maximum was twenty-five kilos. After that, people calmed down. Göth said, "You have time. Go home and pack up and come back and stand again in line of your firm." Of course, regardless of whether they trusted or did not trust him, people had no choice as machine guns were positioned in the *Umschlagplatz* and around the ghetto. I thought to myself, I had friends in the *Judenrat*, which was located outside the *Umschlagplatz* on the right side of where I and everybody stood. I was able to sneak out; in other words, I vanished, though it was dangerous to step out of the row. I went to the *Judenrat*. At the *Judenrat* I learned that they were able to accommodate two hundred people as the so-called cleaning crew, since there remained so much furniture, dishes, and porcelain from Jews who had been deported and which they did not take with them. As I stepped out of the row, Józef Balzer's *mosiek* , who had a son of perhaps eleven or twelve years of age, saw me go in the direction of the Jewish Council. As he saw me step out, he took his son and hid him under his long *bekishe* (long black coat worn by Hassidic Jews), since it was not allowed to have kept children. As noted before, the ghetto was already *Kinderrein*. He followed me into the building of the *Judenrat*, where we were told that two hundred people could remain as a cleaning crew.

People then came with their backpacks and various other belongings they dragged along. There were people who had still been able to save their children and who instead of carrying their baggage, brought children put to sleep with Luminal (a kind of sleeping medication). If they were older, the children were

---

1   "*Niemanden wird ein Haar gekrümmt warden*"; literal translation: "No one's hair will be bent."

instructed to keep quiet. Instead of their belongings they placed their children in their backpacks.

Obersturmbandführer (German equivalent of lieutenant colonel) Göth then announced that we had to place ourselves in rows of four in front of the building.[2] I placed myself in the first half of the row. There were perhaps six hundred women and men. Among them was also Haskel Hollender. He was related to the vice president of the Jewish Council. The *mosiek* of Józef Balzer placed himself in the row not far from me. He covered his son with the *bekishe*. We watched as the Gestapo was leading groups of people for deportation. Tailors, as well as experts in clothing manufacturing, were sent to Płaszów. People were rounded up from their hiding places with sniffing-dogs and sent for deportation. Then came Commander Göth and he noticed that there was twice the number of people that he had allowed, namely two hundred. Women were placed in a wooden shacklike structure while we men stood outside. Göth, the chief of the Gestapo, started to count—one, two, three, four, five, six, and up to perhaps three hundred or four hundred people—and then motioned for those people to march off for deportation. Fortunately, I remained in the so-called cleaning crew. The others were led away for deportation. And then members of the Gestapo came to the women in the wooden shack. Göth and his assistant announced that he needed ten to twenty women who sewed well. So, women volunteered—even employees of the Jewish Council who had sewn in clothing manufacturing. He proceeded to select twenty of these volunteers, told the rest to remain, and sent the volunteers for deportation. Later, we went into the wooden shack. There was a small window, and I looked out to see what was happening, as the windows overlooked the *Umschlagplatz*. I saw my friend and his wife, Eddie Blumenkrantz and Estera, who were the last to be led away.[3] They were the last to go, and then they were gone.

We remained, officially two hundred people, as the cleaning crew. Two or three hours later the Latvian police, the black-clad soldiers from Płaszów, arrived with their trucks. They loaded up all the baggage that the deported Jews

---

2 Dad must have come back from the Jewish Council when people came back with their baggage.

3 The Blumenkrantz were our parents' very good friends. Mother always talked about Estera. Their daughter, Lilusia, survived the war in a convent. She now lives in Israel.

were supposed to have taken with them, each entitled to twenty-five kilos. Ten or twenty trucks arrived, and the goods were dumped in a large warehouse, located on Szpitalna Street, which used to be a metal wholesale place. This location was close to where the Osterweils used to live. We, the cleaning crew, were ordered to sort out the goods: tablecloth to tablecloth, bedsheet to bedsheet, suit to suit, and so forth and to pack them and send them to Germany. The train, which was supposed to go to Płaszów from the train station, went to Auschwitz instead. The Gestapo had told the Jews that they should drop off their baggage, under the pretext that it would be very crowded on the train, as there was not much space. So everybody dropped off their baggage, except those who were hiding children. They were scared to do so. Those criminals were experts. When someone wanted to smuggle himself or herself out with a backpack, they arrested the man, woman, or couple, because they knew that there was a child in it.

They then took all those who had hidden their children and loaded them up on the half trucks and brought them to the ghetto.[4] I saw with my own eyes through the window as they were all shot to death—the mothers with the children—slaughtered. It is impossible to imagine. I saw my good friend Hessig Bissinger, who was a sports teacher at a Jewish sport league called Samson. He was a wonderful person. He was a dental technician by profession and had a beautiful wife and two handsome children. They were all mowed down. It was totally unimaginable and I saw it with my own very eyes. These eyes saw it.[5] And of course, there were many dead, including those taken out from various hiding places. There was no train and it was not worth their while to order a train to Auschwitz. So the Germans placed all the stragglers in the middle (presumable of the *Umschlagplatz*), surrounded by machine gun, and slaughtered them all. Those found in hiding places were encircled in a wire fence. Machine guns were set up, and they fired away—be-be-be-be-be (sound of machine guns)—and slaughtered them all. Then Jews loaded the dead on horse-drawn wagons, covered them with *talesim* (prayer shawls), and took them to the cemetery.

---

4 Dad must be referring to Jews who were arrested outside the *Umschlagplatz*. Dad may have misspoken and meant *Umschlagplatz* rather than ghetto.

5 Dad is crying, pointing to his eyes.

I had gotten hold of identification papers for a married couple and their child by the name of Ślusarczyk and for myself the husband, as Józef Ślusarczyk. I was scared to hold on to them since if they were discovered; it would have meant death with 100 percent certainty. I hid the IDs in the attic of the house where I lived (in the *Judenrat* building, we assume). They were tucked away in a corner to be picked up when it became clear that I had to run from there. That house where I lived had rooms in which thirty people slept, two or three people per bed. There were millions of fleas jumping around, because there was nobody to do the washing and cleaning, as everybody had to go to work. The only places with a laundry were in the hospital or the *Judenrat*, and not available for ordinary workers. One day I went upstairs to the attic to look for the IDs, but they were gone. Most likely, they had been eaten by rats, as there was no shortage of rats. There were also worms, cockroaches, and other insects in addition to millions of fleas.[6]

I wanted to notify my wife that I was alive. I thought to myself that I would not have any possibilities to do so if I remained in the ghetto. I was working in the Jewish canteen when they announced that they were looking for volunteers to bring food to the cemetery for those who were burying the dead. So, I volunteered, as I thought I would find someone whom I could give a note to my contact man, a certain man by the name of Urban. I trusted Urban. I wanted to notify him that I was alive and ask for him to help me.

I asked for two pots of *Ersatzkaffee* (coffee substitute) and some bread and took it to the cemetery for the people (other Jews) who were digging the graves. We were led to the cemetery by a Gestapo member. The Gestapo had to give the grave diggers something to eat, as they dug mass graves, which was very hard work. This was the only humanitarian act by the Gestapo—to order the kitchen to send food to the grave diggers. I volunteered to deliver the food in order to be able to inform Marian Urban, my contact person. I arrived at the cemetery and saw a huge number of corpses being buried. I saw there my own aunt Gella Verderber and her son, both dead. She was shot because she was ill. They had been in my hiding place. They were killed during the roundup of the

---

6   Dad must be referring to his ID since Mom and Felicia had already left the ghetto with their own IDs.

ghetto, where they were shot to death. When I came to the cemetery I gave the workers coffee and bread. The place was packed with Gestapo men who supervised the digging. I saw a girl among the dead who was still alive. Somebody told a Gestapo that the girl was still moving. I cannot forget how the Gestapo came, took a look, and took a Browning and shot her once or twice and killed her.

I sat down on the bench and a Gestapo came to me and said, "You, you go and work the graves." This I did not want to do, since I had heard that after everybody was buried, the grave diggers themselves were also killed and thrown into the graves. I became very scared and said, "*Herr Scharführer*" (German military rank, roughly equivalent to sergeant)—I don't remember what rank he was, and besides I could never figure out ranks among the Gestapo—"I work in the kitchen, and I worked all night long and came here only to bring bread and something to drink for the workers." He yelled at me, "Get lost and go to work," which was overheard by two other Gestapo men. One of them was named Jung (or Novak); the other one was a blond guy. So I took a shovel and I started to dig. The two Gestapo men came by; I approached them and said, "Listen, your colleague just put me to work here, but I worked all night in the kitchen and brought food and drinks for the workers." I asked them to let me go back to the ghetto as I was in no physical shape to continue to work. And they asked, "Is there going to be a bottle of vodka for us?" I said yes, though I did not have any but assumed that I could get a bottle for them. And they said, "OK, come," and they led me back to the ghetto. I was lucky. With regard to the note for Urban, I gave a Christian boy a piece of paper and gave him few *złotys*. I instructed him to go to Nowodąbrowska Street, number so-and-so, where Marian Urban lived, in order to give him a sign that I was still alive.

Incidentally, I still vividly remember three or four sergeants standing around and looking at the cemetery through a fence, when a Gestapo approached them from the other side of the fence and asked, "What are you staring at? Do you want to be in there?" And they vanished, since they were scared. Even highranking officers were scared of the Gestapo.

They led me back to the ghetto. I don't remember if I got the vodka, but that is not important now. There was great misery and wailing in the ghetto.

We had to sort out the clothes and the linen belonging to Jews. I saw my own furniture there. I saw our sofa there. And so it went. Now they started to liquidate the people of the cleaning crew.

I remained officially in the ghetto, but there were people in hiding who were there illegally and who disappeared whenever there was a *Rapport* (roll call), so that there would be the correct number of two hundred people.

I went ahead and wrote a letter to my wife through our contact person, letting her know that my Aryan ID, the one by the name of Józef Ślusarczyk, was worthless and that she should procure for me new identification papers, since she had contact there with people who arranged these matters. She went ahead and sent me papers, which were forged of course, via our contact person, Marian Urban. The IDs stated that my name was Józef Ślusarczyk and that I was a warehouse superintendent in a silk factory in Milanówek. In addition, she sent a blank form letter that was signed and had an official stamp accompanied by appropriate text that had to be filled out. As my wife did not know when I would be leaving, she could not complete the letter.[7] The letter was supposed to show the date and location, name, date of birth, and it said, "Józef Ślusarczyk, as noted in the ID card, is employed by us as a warehouse superintendent and is traveling on our orders to procure raw material and other necessary items. The German authorities are being asked to help him with transportation." That is what I was supposed to type on this blank, signed piece of paper, which had a stamp of the silk company. I was supposed to do that one or two days before my departure.

After the liquidation of the ghetto there were just a small number of people left. We were together in this room and I overheard a young woman, a lawyer, say that she had the opportunity to go and stay with some Aryans. I also over-heard a young man say that he still had two children and a wife alive and that he knew of a Christian family where they could stay, but that he could not get out. He said that he would pay any amount if he could find a car to get out. I had an agreement with Skorupka that should I need to escape, his son would take me, just as he had taken my wife out of town. I just could not listen to this and do nothing. My conscience bothered me. Here I could save a family; I had

---

7   Furthermore, the ID could not be typed on two different typewriters, which would be suspicious.

the possibility to provide him with the means to leave. So I thought about this for a while and called him to another room and said: "Listen, if you swear to me on the life of your children that you will not disclose this to anyone, I will give you an address and give you a possibility to leave and save you and your family." He kissed my hands and swore by the life of his children and his wife and his gassed parents that he would not mention this to anyone. So I gave him the address where to find Skorupka, which was right across from the ghetto. There was a garment manufacturing shop that also provided for the military. They made suits and other clothing. It was really a tailor outfit. The boss was a certain Mr. Madritch. There he would find a businessman named Skorupka, a *Scheigiz* (Yiddish term for a gentile) with light blond hair. He lived there in the garage with his father. I told him to use my name and to tell him that I had sent him. I also told him to negotiate with Skorupka. He swore to me that he would not mention it to anyone. And indeed he got in touch with Skorupka's son. One evening in November, I believe, it was already dark, around 9 p.m., when I met this young man (whom I had told about Skorupka) in the ghetto. He said to me, "Keep your fingers crossed. The boys left for Czechoslovakia. There was a redheaded guy and four other boys. Skorupka was the chauffeur." Their plan was to have a friend of Skorupka's who had an old motorcycle drive ahead of them to make sure that there were no road blocks and that the air was clear. They were supposed to drive via Nowy Sącz to the Czechoslovakian border with Hungary. I told him, "This is a chutzpah of you. I gave you the opportunity to save your family. You cried that you wanted to save your family. You deceived me. Now you tell me of five boys who drove off." He said he did not want to take the risk and that one of the boys was to return with Skorupka after dropping off the four boys in Czechoslovakia. That boy would then drive him later on to the border.

When I heard this I did not go back to the place where I was supposed to sleep. I said to the brother of Osterweil who also worked at Madritch, "Heschek, you are going to Madritch anyway," where he had to take apart machines and cut up other material, all of which was to be sent to Płaszów. "Please see if the shop is open," since Madritch was the sole proprietor of the mountings and fittings business and had no other employees.[8] The shop was in a courtyard and was not facing the street. The house was a *Durchgangshaus* (walk-through house). I said to Osterweil, "I will expect you at noon." I decided not to stand for roll call anymore, as I was scared that something could happen. At 12:00 p.m., the workers of the cleaning crew went to eat. The workplace where they sorted out goods was only about two hundred to three hundred steps from the entrance to the ghetto. So, I waited at the entrance to the ghetto, and I asked Heschek what was going on. "It is closed," he said. "Oy vey," I said. "If it is closed and it is lunchtime, then something happened." And I took off right away. I realized that if Skorupka and the men were caught, a catastrophe might happen. My name would come up and Skorupka and the men would tell them that I referred them to him. That meant a 100 percent death sentence. So I took off and went up to the attic,[9] where there was a small hole from which I could see the *Umschlagplatz*. Incidentally, there was another man in the attic who was in hiding. We both looked out, and I told him the story. I saw as both gates opened and three horse-drawn carriages full of Gestapos rode in. The carriages had belonged to Jews. The Gestapos dismounted. There was a roll call and everybody was standing in two rows. Everyone was ordered to raise his hand holding up his ID. The Gestapos never asked for your name, but instead ordered people to show their identification cards. And they walked around inspecting the IDs. I said to the man who was hiding with me in the attic, "Oh my God, they are looking for me."

To this day I am not certain if they were looking for me, though it was highly unusual for the Gestapo to come in the evening and in such large numbers. Anyway, we saw how they went through all the double lines and inspected all the IDs and then went back to the carriages and left. Since they did not find anyone, I assumed they were looking for me. By this time the Michalewicz House was outside the ghetto because the Germans shrunk and redrew the ghetto borders after every deportation, so I did not live there anymore. In the *Judenrat* thirty to forty people lived in one room, which was flea infested. So I went to the laundry room and hid in this rather primitive hiding place. The

8 Unclear: above he is noted to be the boss of a textile shop.
9 Most likely of the *Judenrat*.

man in the attic showed me where the laundry room was, which was downstairs. The laundry room was full of sand and dirt. The man lifted some sandbags and arranged a hiding place for me. I stayed there all night long and did not move. I was scared they would come at night again to look for me at my usual sleeping place, which was the flea-infested room in the Jewish Council.

By the way, it was common at night to hear the noise of metal hooves of horse-drawn carriages. When they would stop in front of a house, everybody's heart would stand still. Everybody was scared because the Gestapos would drag out two or three people and shoot them right in front of the house. They did that during the night. Sometimes, it was because somebody was reported; or some other reason. We hid and sat quiet as a mouse (literally: like a mouse under a broom).

📑 Historical Notes

The Final Liquidation, September 1943. The Holocaust Research Project website gives an in-depth description of this tragic event.

> In the middle of August 1943 a conference was held in the office of SS-*Obergruppenführer* Wilhelm Koppe in Kraków. ... [I] t was announced that a fourth Aktion would take place in early September 1943 to liquidate the Tarnów ghetto. SS-*Oberführer* Scherner took a particularly sinister and deadly decision by placing SS-*Hauptsturmführer* Amon Göth, the liquidator of the ghettos in Lublin, Rzeszow, Bochnia, Przemysl, and Kraków, and the Szebnie camp, in charge of the operation.
>
> At the end of August 1943 a further conference was held to fine-tune the plans for the final liquidation of the ghetto. 200 Jewish men and 100 Jewish women were to remain in the ghetto to serve as a cleaning-up party. 2,000 Jews from the Madritsch clothing factory were transferred to Plaszów. The approximately 6,000 remaining Jews were to receive "special treatment" in Auschwitz-Birkenau.
>
> On the morning of 3 September 1943 SS/SD and other forces surrounded the ghetto. The working Jews from Ghetto A paraded as on any other day, the Jews in Ghetto B also gathered in the Magdeburger Platz. The Jewish clearing command was organized and made to parade in the grounds of the Singer crate factory, which proved to be extremely suitable for the purpose because it was already fenced. A sentry was posted at the entrance to the factory grounds to prevent Jews selected for deportation from slipping into the rear cleaning party; next followed the selection of Jews from Ghetto A for employment at the Plaszów forced labor camp.
>
> Many Jews realized that the Jews in the Singer factory grounds were not slated for immediate deportation and tried to join them. Göth and his colleagues had anticipated this move, and set about

ill-treating the Jews who attempted to escape. Göth walked through the rows of Jews with his pistol drawn, shouting and dealing out blows. He immediately shot dead some Jews who were slow to act. He hit a Jewish woman called Zimmermann so hard that she fell to the ground, dead. Jews were shot out of hand and their bodies strewn across the square.

Jews hiding in their houses were shot on the spot. That same afternoon, Jews were led in groups from Magdeburger Platz to the railway station and loaded into goods wagons, 160 Jews per wagon. The air-vents of the wagons were closed and wooden planks nailed over them. Many Jews died of suffocation en route to Auschwitz, due to the lack of ventilation.

About 50 Jews who had attempted to smuggle small children with them out of the ghetto in rucksacks were taken out of the transport and driven back by lorry to the ghetto, where Göth and other SS-men started shooting at them. They were all killed."

Holocaust Research Project, "Tarnow Ghetto," http://www.holocaustresearch-project.org/ghettos/tarnow.html.

Escape from the Tarnów Ghetto

After that incident, I recognized that the ground was burning under my feet. So I took out my papers along with the blank form. Though the business of Jósef Balzer had been liquidated, I went there with the group, as they had a typewriter. I did not know how to type, so I asked my fellow sufferers who knew how to type, and one man from Lemberg came forward. I confided in him and went to the *mosiek*, who supervised our work. The *mosiek* was actually *ein Stück Kapo*.[1] He used to beat people, including children. This particular *mosiek* was privileged. He himself did not work. He would buy black-market items, such as cloth, and supply the commissioner with those goods. I entered a room that looked like an office. The *mosiek* stood there with his *tallis* and *tefillin* and prayed. He prayed *Shmoneh Esreh* (silent devotion prayer), a prayer during which one is not allowed to talk. So, I waited out of respect, as he considered himself an assistant commissioner. When he finished praying and took off his *tefillin*, I asked him if he would allow me to write something on the typewriter. He asked me, "What do you want to write?" I told him, "Something which is a matter of life and death for me." He said that he must see what it is. I said, "What does it matter to you?" He opened the door and pushed me out and locked the door and said, "Not in my shop." I wanted to give him fifty American dollars, which was a lot of money during wartime. When he refused, I offered him one hundred dollars, as my life depended on it. And again he said,

---

1 This is a derogatory term meaning a "piece of *Kapo*." A *Kapo* was a prisoner who worked inside Nazi concentration camps in certain lower administrative positions. There were Jewish *Kapos* who were known to be especially cruel to their co-religionists.

"Not in my shop." That was his answer; from an Orthodox Jew. I could not start a fight with him. Besides I was scared that he would tell the commissioner, who could immediately send the Gestapo, and then I would be done for. After all, he was a *Kapo*. Incidentally, he died here in Antwerp. He did not find much happiness. His son went to Israel and was shot to death by Arabs during his first year over there. He survived by going to Hungary. Later, he went to live in Bad Nauheim (a resort town in Germany), where he claimed to be a rabbi, and then wound up here in Antwerp, where he worked in the diamond exchange. I never talked to him. He was a miserable animal.

Anyway, I returned to the ghetto empty-handed as he had not allowed me to use the typewriter, and therefore I could not leave for Warsaw. Someone told me to go to Goldhammer Street, located in the middle of town. Over there was another office of Józef Balzer and since I was an employee of Mr. Balzer, I thought I would be able to use their typewriter. But here the conditions were much worse than in the other Balzer operation. Over there, in case the commissioner or a Gestapo wanted to enter the premises, they had to ring the bell and the security officer had to open the door. Furthermore, the house was quite isolated and one could see and hear if someone was coming toward it. Therefore, one did not have to fear that the commissioner would come while typing. When we arrived at the other division (on Goldhammer Street), I approached the other assistant commissioner, a very assimilated Jew, who actually did not find out that he was Jewish until the Hitler era. He did not understand Yiddish, spoke only German, as he came from the area of Bielitz (Bielsko-Biala), which was part of what was Silesia, where for the most part German was spoken. I approached him and asked him if he would let me write a letter on the typewriter. His name was Stiel or something like that. "What do you have to type?" he asked. "It is a matter of life and death for me. I have to get out of here. I am concerned that the Gestapo is after me." I then showed him the written text in German, which had to be typed on the official stationary of the firm. He took the text, read it and read it again, and said, "This is written in poor German. Give it to me and I will type it for you the right way." This was the first time that I had ever seen this man and yet he took the paperwork and endangered his life, since the Gestapo could come in at any moment. If caught we would both get a bullet in our heads without any hesitation.[2] And he typed the letter for me in perfect German, since he was a German Jew and had been an accountant and secretary in some business. When he gave me the letter he said, "I wish that your departure should be blessed with a lot of good fortune." He was an angel. I did not have to write the letter. He wrote it for me.

I then went ahead to establish contact with Urban, my trusted courier, who was in contact with my wife. I did not know, nor wanted to know, my wife's address, where she lived, because I feared in case someone reported me to the Gestapo and they tortured me, that I might talk. By not knowing her address, I could not betray her. So, now I had the identification card in the name of Józef Ślusarcyk and the new date and other facts that had been written with the typewriter. I started scheming how to arrange my escape. I wrote a letter and sent it with a messenger boy, asking Urban to come.

By the way, did you read the book *Königshofstrasse*?[3] Just like in the book, my wife had sent me mastic to change my penis to a "gentile" penis. Urban had brought the mastic to me. He brought it to Józef Balzer's place. I told Urban that I did not even know what an uncircumcised penis looked like. So we went to the bathroom and he showed me his penis since I did not even know where to begin. The mastic was similar to a gum preparation (putty-like) in liquid form. Urban showed me that you had to pull the skin above the head of the penis and hold the skin until it got tight. So, in case I was checked to see if I was Jewish, that is whether I was circumcised, I would be safe. Mr. Urban told me that the mastic cost a lot of money, and I gave him the money to buy it.[4]

Our jewelry and watch store had been on the main street of Tarnów, which led to the train station. The railroad employees frequently used to be our customers. They often bought on installment. Say something cost fifty *złotys*; they would pay in installments of five to ten *złotys*, usually after the first of the month. We did this because the management of the railroad frequently bought an Omega or a Doxa (brand of watch) from our store. I was therefore afraid to

---

2 Dad is crying.
3 Felicia was unable to find any information about this book.
4 Conflicting information: did Mother send the mastic or did Urban buy it?

go to the train station, since the railroaders knew me. They could immediately say, "What are you doing here?" and they could call the Gestapo or the police and inform them that I was Jewish. That is why I did not want to board the train in Tarnów. I asked Urban to provide me with a bicycle, which I would ride to the next train station. I also asked him to buy two train tickets to Warsaw, one for him and one for me. That is how I planned for the situation.

Then, I had another idea. I knew a man, Erich Richter who was the second or third commissioner. I went to him and told him, "Mr. Richter, I need to talk to you urgently." "Come up to my apartment," he said. He had two small rooms. "What is going on? Fire away." I told him, "Listen, all I own is sixty thousand *złotys*. I'll give you the sixty thousand *złotys* to drive me to Mościce," which was the name of the next train station outside Tarnów. I suggested that we take a horse-drawn carriage for which I would pay. "As the commissioner, you have the right to drive me there. I have a wife and a child living on Aryan papers in Warsaw." I confided in him because I had seen how good-hearted he was. The worst he ever did to get people to work was to tap them lightly on their knees, to let them know that he was strict. However, he actually was good-hearted, and though I never had any dealings with him, I trusted him. He told me: "What made you think to tell me all this? Don't you know that I can denounce you right away and that you would be dead within an hour?" I told him, "I know that you are only capable of helping a person survive, not to denounce him to the Gestapo." He looked at me and said, "Go out, go to work, and come back in half an hour. I'll think about it." So I went downstairs, and half an hour later I went back up. He told me, "Listen, if we get caught we'll both be dead. They'll find Aryan papers on you and see that you are not wearing the Jewish star. They will hold me as an accomplice, and we will both be in danger. And by the way, the sixty thousand *złotys* that you offered me, you can use them more than I when you get to Warsaw. But I do have an idea. The manager of the house who lives below me is a Christian, and her husband is a railroad worker. He is now on leave. Go downstairs to her and borrow his uniform from her. She should not tell anyone a word about it."

I had a thin summer coat. I put it on and went downstairs. The woman laughed: "What do you need it for?" I said: "Are you afraid I will run away with it? The place is guarded." "No," she said, she was not afraid and gave it to me. She laughed. She did business in the black market and lived off us Jews. She gave me the railroader's hat and the whole uniform. I went upstairs to Richter. "Did anyone see you?" "No," I said. "Take off your clothes and put on the uniform." I put it on. After I had changed he said, "Let me take a look at you. That is how you will travel to Warsaw. Go to the mirror and look at yourself." I went to the mirror. I did not recognize myself. That had been some idea. I would have never thought of it. "Listen, go back downstairs to the woman and borrow the uniform. Her husband is gone on leave for fourteen days. In this uniform nobody will recognize you. That is how you will travel to Warsaw and neither you nor I will be endangered." I went downstairs and made her a proposal. Let's say a railroad worker paid three hundred *złotys* for his uniform, which was discounted since he worked for the Polish railroad, which needed workers. So I proposed it to her. She said that she could not do it. "Listen, I'll give you as much as you want and I'll bring it back, or send it back."

"If you give me five thousand *złotys*, then I'll be sure that you'll send it back." I accepted. I took the uniform and went upstairs. In the meantime I had set up a meeting with Urban, my contact person, who was to bring me a bicycle. I would then ride it to Mościce, the next railway station, clad in my uniform. He also was to give me the train tickets, which had to be purchased at the main train station in Tarnów, a place I did not want to go. He was to buy two tickets and take me to my wife. He knew her address. I did not. And that is what happened. When the group, which consisted of twenty to thirty people, left the ghetto led by a guard, I positioned myself and the bicycle in the middle among the group. I had put on my uniform. Our group saw the bicycle, but the guard did not notice it. We were in a rather wide street and I had placed my coat over me, the cap hidden under the coat, when I snuck out from the row of the group. I unbuttoned my coat, put the cap on, got on the bike, and took off.

I had the identification papers in the name of Ślusarczyk describing him as a manager of a silk factory; yet, I was clad in a railroader's uniform. I had been unable to obtain the proper ID as a railroader, since I had to get out of the ghetto in a great hurry. As I got outside of town, I saw a checkpoint manned by police who were stopping every peasant, male and female. My heart was racing while I thought of what to do. I, of course, adjusted my coat so that my uniform was visible, hoping that they would have respect for the uniform. They let me pass without asking any questions and waved me through without having to identify myself.[5]

I arrived by bicycle at the train station, and as planned, Urban stood next to a tree on the platform where the train stopped. That is how I knew where he would be. The bicycle did not belong to Urban but was borrowed from a neighbor. I was to lean the bike against the tree and the owner would pick it up later. Everything was coordinated for it to work out. And indeed, the train arrived on time and after it stopped, Urban stepped onto the platform. As I boarded the train, he slipped the train ticket in my pocket and boarded himself. We did not sit together because he did not want to endanger himself; neither did I want to endanger him. We acted like two strangers. By the way, the train was full. Meanwhile, there was a police check on the train. They were looking for smugglers and smuggled items. People used to smuggle butter, meat, and other items. They were apparently checking peasants for smuggled items, but I did not know this at first, and I was afraid that they would ask for my ID stating that I was a railroad worker. I knew that railroad workers got tickets at half or quarter off, sometimes even for free, and yet I had a fully priced ticket. What's more, I had the ID papers of a businessman of a silk factory; yet, I was dressed in a railroader's uniform. So I walked away and threw the cap out of the window of the moving train and covered my uniform with my coat and pulled up my uniform pants, which I had put on over another pair of pants, which were knickers and were in vogue. I looked up thinking that they had noticed something, and I was quite scared. But I was lucky; they did not come to me. The bottom legs of the knickers were usually held in place with a rubber band or buttons. Mine were held up with rubber bands and I had fleas dancing in my pants, fleas that I had brought from the ghetto. The fleas tickled and bit, yet I had to hold still. They were trapped in my pant legs and could not get out

---

5   Note from Felicia: "I remember Dad talking about this incident. When he saw the checkpoint, he at first did not know what to do. He thought of running away, but this would have tipped off the police that he had something to hide, so he decided to just bluff it and keep on riding."

because of the rubber band. Occasionally I pulled on the rubber bands to let them out. That was in October 1943, after the final liquidation of the ghetto. There remained officially two hundred cleaning-crew members.

 # Life in Warsaw as an Aryan

Urban took me to the apartment where my wife lived in Warsaw. Before that she had lived in Milanówek, as well as in Iwonicz-Zdrój, but had to run away from both towns because she was also being blackmailed. Engineer Zigmund Hollender, the man who had helped my wife, was being blackmailed, and he had to get away. All his possessions had been taken away from him by the blackmailers, and he was afraid that they would send the Gestapo after him. My wife lived in his apartment and therefore also had to get away. My wife had managed to procure a reserve apartment in Warsaw and that is where she moved to.[1] The two girls whose life I had saved and for whom I got the fur coats also lived in that apartment. They too had been blackmailed, despite their great looks, meaning without any trace of Semitic appearance. They had gotten a room to live in through a contact person and later were blackmailed. They were robbed of everything. I do not know whether they were beaten up or not.

Whenever an apartment was exposed through extortion, one had to move out because one never knew whether the Gestapo had been notified. The underworld got wind that Jewish women lived there, and so the sisters had to move. Blackmail was a daily occurrence. The blackmailers would simply approach you if they suspected that you were a Jew, whether you had a Jewish appearance or not. They always moved in pairs dressed like spies with officers' boots. When they saw a young man they would approach him on the street from both sides and say: "You are Jewish." "What? What are you talking about?" They would

---

1 Many people had a second apartment in reserve, just in case one became compromised.

say, "Come inside the house and drop your pants." If the person was indeed a Jew, they would rob him and demand to be taken to his apartment, where they would rob him of everything. Sometimes, they were actually real spies who worked for the Gestapo, in which case they would first rob their victims and then take them to the Gestapo and hand them over. That was a daily occurrence.

Urban took me to my wife. I came in and my wife could not comprehend that I had survived. "No, no," she said, "I was told that you were dead." She even had gone to a psychic and had shown her my picture and was told, "No, this man is dead." My wife had heard through the underground organization that the Tarnów ghetto had been liquidated and that not a single Jew had survived. She was convinced that she was a widow, that I was no longer alive. I sent Urban to buy vodka on the black market. Also present was Stefan Klara, an engineer, also a Jew under false identity. His real name was Jesefort. His father had been the respected president of the chamber of commerce in Kraków. I do not remember the father's first name anymore. Between the three of us, we drank a liter of vodka to celebrate our success.

Now, I did not want to give up my railroader's uniform, because it was the best and safest protection whenever I wanted to go out. I could be 90 to 95 percent certain that no one would accuse me of being Jewish, because no one would look closely at me, not even blackmailers. Even they would not dare to approach me while in uniform.

Meanwhile the underground organization had been notified that an ID was needed for me.

When I was still in Tarnów, Natalka Hubler, the older of the two sisters, had sent a birth certificate in the name of Andrzej Białecki via a messenger to me in the ghetto. The birth certificate was intended for her lover, a man by the name of Jacub Birnbaum (his nickname was Kuba). Kuba, whom I had saved in the bunker, had been a high official in the Jewish community in Cologne. Today (1981) he has a very large clothing store in Cologne. I was to give him the birth certificate and tell him to go to Warsaw. Kuba was behind a wired enclosure (some kind of confinement set up by the Germans). I called him over. I said, "Kuba, Natalka sent you this birth certificate so that you can get out and live on Aryan papers. She has a place for you to live." He said, "Schlomek, what sense does it make for me to go as a Pole with Aryan papers with a name like Andrzej Białecki, when I do not speak Polish. If somebody stops me and talks to me, I'll be doomed immediately. I will go to Plaszów." Kuba was born and raised in Cologne, but his parents were Polish and therefore considered foreigners. That is why he and his parents were expelled to Poland during the war. He had been in the garment business, and the Germans needed people in the garment industry to sew and cut uniforms for the military. Not knowing any Polish, Kuba did not want to go to Warsaw and thought that he had a better chance of surviving in the ghetto. Indeed, he survived in Plaszów, a labor camp near Kraków. He told me to hold on to the birth certificate. So I was left with the birth certificate of Andrzej Białecki, but I had no other documents in this name. I only had documents in the name of Józef Ślusarczyk, a manager of a silk factory in Milanówek, and I arrived in Warsaw with them.

I knew a man who had contact with the underground organization called AK, short for *Armia Krajowa*, which means Home Army. AL was another underground organization of Socialists and Communists. This man had procured the birth certificate for Birnbaum, but Kuba had not wanted it, so it stayed with me. The man said that the birth certificate was supposedly authentic and that he would get me the corresponding identification card and documents, specifying that I was a railroad worker by profession, along with a certification that I worked for the railroad. He also bought me a railroader's cap, as I had thrown mine out of the train to Warsaw, and I did not dare go out on the street without a uniform. The man's appearance was much more Aryan than mine. He came up to our room in order to take care of the identification papers in the name of Andrzej Białecki, as well as an ID as a railroader, a Polish railroader, since there were also German railroaders.[2] The German railroaders had golden buttons on their uniform. The Polish railroaders' uniform had white or metallic buttons; I am not sure which. The German railroaders were always in charge, as they had higher positions. So Zigmund Hollender came to my place with the papers and the stuff for taking fingerprints and then handed them over to the

---

2 Unclear who this man with the contact to the underground was, but he likely was Jewish as Dad says he had Aryan appearance.

man with contact to the underground. With my new cap, I could get out from time to time when no one was home. And that is how I moved about Warsaw as an Aryan.

And now a new chapter started: life in Warsaw with Aryan papers. We held so-called penis shows, in which we were shown how an uncircumcised penis actually looked. Women would turn their heads away. Let me tell a story with regard to this issue. Though tragic, it had a good ending. It was Christmas and we, of course, decorated a Christmas tree and sang Christmas songs in Polish. This took place in my apartment. There was a big crowd and among them was a Jew in a railroad uniform, but as opposed to me, he actually worked for the railroad. We sang for our neighbors' sake and drank schnapps. After the police curfew Stefan Klara came running asking if there was a doctor present and that it absolutely had to be a Jewish doctor. He wanted to know if one was present among us. There was none in our company. And here is what he told us happened. He had been at another Christmas party, also a Jewish one, where they had put on the same show with a Christmas tree. It was common for Jewish men to undergo surgery in which the skin of their penis was stretched over the head of the penis and then sewn in place. This was done because it turned out that the mastic or putty used to make circumcised penises appear uncircumcised was useless. First of all the putty was diluted in a liquid that burned when applied to the head of the penis. And then, when it became warm the skin retracted back slowly. So there was this man with his wife at that party, who was quite drunk. He went to the back room and wanted to have sexual relations with her. He had undergone this surgery and the stitches broke. His penis swelled up tremendously, and he was in agony. I do not know how the story ended, but I think the swelling went down, and all ended well.

Many men underwent that type of surgery because the blackmailers were a scourge, whether you were a Jew or not. I want to tell you a story that I personally overheard. I was riding in the streetcar, obviously in my conductor's uniform, and since all seats were taken I held on to the straps. A young woman boarded and a man stood next to her, holding on to the straps. They greeted each other and I could not help but overhear their conversation, which was not particularly interesting. At one point the woman asked the man, in Polish, of course, "Excuse me, can you tell me what time it is?" He said, "Unfortunately not. I can't tell you. I was walking on Gaczgebot Street [3] when two men approached me, one from the right and one from the left side. They claimed that I was a Jew and ordered me to go with them to a house to check if I was circumcised. Since I had nothing to fear, I went with them and let down my pants. They checked and saw that I was not circumcised. Yet, despite that, they took my watch, my wedding ring, my pen, and all the *złotys* I had in my pocket." And then he whispered to her, but I could still hear it: "I used to be an officer in the Polish army, and those thugs are looking for officers. But I did not reveal this, and they let me go."

So even when they were wrong about the identity, they still stole. That was their profession. It was commonly said, "Stupid you. Why should you work? How much can you make? Go to the streets; if you find a Jew, you won't have to work for the rest of your life." That was the topic of conversation. There was a hunt for Jews who had survived. I am not talking about the Jews who were caught and handed over and who did not survive. I heard unbelievable stories. There was hardly a person who had not been blackmailed, robbed, and beaten up.

My wife had a good friend by the name of Wanda Simka. She was quite removed from Judaism but was a Jewess by birth. She was a lawyer, had finished her studies; but nevertheless she was stupid. One day she came up to our place and said that she had to go to a gynecologist and that she was embarrassed because she was not a virgin. She was married but had papers as a single person, so my wife loaned her her wedding band, the one I gave her when we got married. And she, her sister, and a male friend were mugged and beaten up. They stole the wedding band my wife had loaned her. All this because she, an academician, was ashamed that she was not a virgin. There are all kinds of people. I was very angry at my wife. It was idiotic of that woman. Who cared whether she was married when going to the doctor? Did she have to show that she was married?

As I mentioned, I landed in Warsaw with my messenger and contact person, Marian Urban, who took me upstairs to my wife with me following behind him. She had a place, which was a small room. She lived there with our

---

3   We could not find record of this street.

child. The room was in a family house, which actually used to be for bigwigs of the Warsaw magistrate. However, during the war each room of the building housed an entire family. There were several such single-family houses. My wife paid a deposit for the room (literally: key money). Next door lived a streetcar conductor with his family, I believe with three children. Further down on the same floor lived a certain Mrs. Stasia. She was a smuggler who smuggled butter and groceries to Łódź and other towns and from there to the German Reich. She then smuggled other goods from there back to Warsaw. She trusted my wife, Zofia, with the key to her apartment. Below us lived a woman with her mother-in-law. So, in all, four families lived in the house.

My wife's name was still Ślusarczyk, and I was now Andrzej Białecki. I lived in my wife's place. In the corner of the room was a wardrobe. We moved the wardrobe in such a manner that it became a hiding place. I slept and lived in the room, which accommodated five people, a room which was of the size of a small office. The two sisters slept in some sort of a bed, and the three of us, my wife and child and I, slept in another bed. My wife and child slept at the head of the bed and I at the foot of the bed. That is how we lived until the Polish uprising in Warsaw. From time to time when no one was in the house, I went out to buy something to eat. My wife did not dare to go out because of her black hair. Before my arrival, the two sisters had taken care of that. They had been blackmailed in their previous apartment, and as they knew my wife's address, they just sort of planted themselves in the room. My wife had given the deposit to a Polish landlady, a certain Mrs. Dąbrowska. If I remember correctly it was twenty-five thousand *złotys*. But my wife had not yet registered with the police as the owner of the apartment. When the two sisters moved in, Dąbrowska told my mother, "Zofia, you have to register," since Dąbrowska had moved out and given the room to my wife. My wife answered, "You can register it on your name." So Dąbrowska went to the magistrate and registered that she lived and had an apartment on Szucha 11 and registered all those who also lived there.[4] It was common for people to sublet rooms in their apartments. There was no construction going on, and people came to Warsaw from surrounding areas to submerge or to improve their standard of living due to better earning

---

4   Presumably referring to the two sisters. Unclear in whose name Dąbrowska registered Mom.

potential. As a result, there were no apartments available, and it was quite common among Poles to have five or six people live in one room. By the time I came to Warsaw, it was completely *Judenrein* (clean of Jews). The Jewish ghetto in Warsaw had been totally bombed and burned out. That had occurred several months before I came to Warsaw, which was in October of 1943, and I think the Jewish (Warsaw) ghetto was liquidated in May or June. From time to time, we saw through the window an SS man or a policeman lead a group of people to work still wearing the Jewish star. We did not know what the significance of that was what these people did, where they were going or lived. Certainly, they did not live in the Warsaw ghetto because the ghetto had been completely liquidated.[5]

Zigmund Hirsch had also been blackmailed in the street, despite his good looks (referring to Aryan appearance).[6] He had a colleague who sublet a room at a *Volksdeutsche's* home, of course, as an Aryan. They had to get up at 6:30 a.m. to be at work at 7:30 or 8:00. Hirsch came to his friend's place every day around lunchtime, where there was a radio owned by the *Volksdeutsche*. Hirsch always brought news from the front transmitted by the English-language broadcasts, since the German broadcast never transmitted the truth. Hirsch came every day at 1:00 to my wife under the pretext that he was a friend of our neighbor. I would then crawl out of my hiding place and we played cards to kill time until the curfew. In wintertime the curfew was already at 3:30, 4:30, or 5:00 p.m., and in summer it was at 7:00 or 8:00 p.m. The curfew was instituted to protect the Germans after the underground had killed off some Gestapo bigwigs. Zigmund Hirsch always left half an hour before the curfew to go to his apartment. One night, in the middle of the night, he came running to us and slept over in our room, petrified because the Gestapo had come to where he was living. He had managed to crawl out through a back door or window. He came and slept at our place until he was able to obtain another place, which most likely the underground organization, the AK or *Armia Krajowa* got for him. And that is the way we lived.

---

5 After the Warsaw ghetto uprising, April 19 to May 16, 1943, the ghetto was burned. Jewish prisoners were used to clean up the ghetto area after its destruction.

6 It is unclear who Zigmund Hirsch was, but he appears to be an acquaintance or friend.

Zigmund Hollender, who had been threatened with extortion in Mila-nówek, came to Warsaw and joined the anti-Semitic underground organization called AL, which stood for *Armja Ludowa* (People's Army) where he worked as an engineer. The underground operated as follows: They decided on a target, such as a bigwig of the Gestapo or SS. The underground then sent schoolgirls to observe when he would go to the office, when he went to lunch, which street he used, and so forth. These schoolgirls with their school backpacks, maybe twelve or thirteen years old, observed these events and wrote them down. Then the underground sent Zigmund Hollender to devise a plan at what spot to shoot him dead, to assassinate him. He always planned it out and when it was ready and the date set, he would come to our place and say, "Andrzej and Zofia, do not go out tomorrow," because the Germans would take reprisal actions; they would take hostages, say one hundred or two hundred of them, beat them up, and shoot them. So, he would always advise us when not to go out. My wife did not go out anyway, but I would go out from time to time. I don't remember whether the two sisters were already gone. They were rarely home because they had girlfriends who also lived on Aryan papers. The assassins would come by horse-drawn carriage, which were rare. Usually, people used streetcars or some sort of rickshaw. Many converted bicycles into rickshaws, which were used to bring people to the train station, as well as to pick up passengers. Cars as well as horses had been confiscated so that the rickshaws were the best mode of transportation. Usually, whenever the rickshaw drivers suspected that they had a Jewish man or woman as a passenger, they did the job themselves.[7]

When nobody was home or if I had to go out to shop, I put on my uniform and took the identification card. As a railroader, one had to have an extra identification card, which required a monthly stamp, stating the first to the last day of the month. The railroaders could also go out at night in spite of the police curfew because they rode into town from somewhere at night and they had to get home. But I never took advantage of that opportunity because I had no interest in going out at night.

---

7 Meaning that the drivers blackmailed them, robbed them, and /or killed them.

📑 Historical Notes

Notes from Felicia:

1. "Father could not live openly in our room as officially he was not Mother's husband and could not register with the Polish police. That was required if you wanted to rent a place. Father was fluent in Yiddish, but his Polish was not good enough to talk to a Polish policeman, who would become suspicious. It was just too dangerous, so Father had to hide behind the wardrobe. As far as the neighbors were concerned, he did not live there. He would come in "to visit," making it known to everyone. He was supposed to be a friend of the family. Then he would leave again, making sure to wave and yell good-bye so that neighbors knew he was leaving. He then would tiptoe back, making sure no one would see him."

2. I remember Mother telling me that she did go out. This was most likely before Dad came to Warsaw. Mother was advised not to take me out with her because I looked too Jewish with my black hair. Since Mother also had black hair, it would have been too noticeable to have two black-haired people together. I also remember Mother telling me this story: One day, she went out to get food and left me home alone. Mother was caught up in a Police roundup but managed to hide. However, she was gone a long time and when she got home, I had fallen asleep crying, as I was scared that Mother would not come back. It seems to me that I remember the fear and see myself lying on the bed crying and being woken by Mother.

Living on Aryan papers. In his book *Secret City: The Hidden Jews of Warsaw, 1940–1945*, Gunnar S. Paulson describes at length the precarious conditions, difficulties, and problems that people "hiding on the surface" were facing. These were especially difficult for the thousands (according to Paulson) of Jews who were living on Aryan papers. Documents printed by the underground were essential for survival in a city under strict Polish and German control. Paulson explains:

It was the Jews in hiding who always had to conquer the greatest difficulties. ... [Even before German occupation] all residents of Warsaw ... were registered in their building's tenancy records as well as the municipal records office. In addition, all Catholics ... were represented in parish birth, baptismal, marriage and death registers. A forged identity document by itself might pass muster in the event of simple street check, but if someone fell under suspicion, the authorities would begin to delve into this whole web of documentation. ... [By] 1943, all non-Germans over the age of nineteen were required to obtain a *Kennkarte* [ID card] through their local record offices. The *Kennkarte* bore a serial number and fingerprints as well as the name, address and photograph of the bearer. ... Document production was carried out by many private entrepreneurs and the Polish underground. ... If a Jew could move about confidently and behave like a Pole—for example, responding to attempted extortion by threatening to call the police—then "bad looks" and many other disabilities could be overcome. But this required extraordinary discipline and self-control. ... A more decisive factor that could identify a Jew was language. Many Jews spoke Polish imperfectly or with a characteristic accent, and even someone whose Polish was perfect might let slip in a characteristically Jewish expression or turn of phrase. One individual, for example, was once recognized as a Jew because he asked, "What street are you from?" where a Pole would have asked, "What district are you from?" ... At the other extreme, Jewishness could be suspected if someone's Polish was too good. ... Many assimilated Jews spoke the language of Mickiewicz [Polish writer/poet], rather than the language of the street. ... Jews living openly as Aryans ... could [often] easily be recognized by building porters or neighbors. The porter Stefan Giemza writes of a certain family, "I could tell at once they were Jews. No one came to see them. They didn't get any letters."

Because there was a strict curfew starting early in the evening, Paulson continues:

> Social life revolved around the courtyard, building, or staircase. ...
> Tenants visited each other, wandering from floor to floor, talking
> about the day's events, sharing news about the political situation,
> and often playing bridge. ...
>
> Nearly every Jewish memoir or testimony ... mentions en-
> counters with *szmalcowniks* [extortionists, blackmailers], and often
> several such encounters. Even the most assimilated and best-inte-
> grated Jews seem to have drawn their attention. ... Blackmailers
> simply demanded everything and were prepared to turn the *melina*
> [slang word used for Jewish clandestine residence] upside-down
> to find it. ... Not only did blackmailers demand huge sums, but
> their appearance meant that a *melina* was "burnt." If the victims
> did not quickly find new accommodation, the blackmailers could
> return, and if the Jews had nothing to pay them with, they might
> be turned over to the police.

Gunnar S. Paulson, *Secret City: The Hidden Jews of Warsaw, 1940–1945* (New
Haven, CT: Yale University Press, 2002), 98–111.

Diane Ackerman, in her book *The Zookeeper's Wife* (New York: Norton &
Company, 2007), explains further that Jews who lived on the surface, not in
hiding, had to "keep up the masquerade at all times. ... The smallest oversight
could give him/her away, for example, not knowing the price of a tram ticket,
appearing too aloof, and not receiving enough letters or visitors, not taking part
in the typical social life of a housing block" (173).

17

A Refuge to Many

My place was virtually a meeting point. The most crucial and critical principle of a "newly created Aryan" was that once that person had an apartment or any kind of shelter, he should never reveal its location to anyone. The reason was the fear that if anybody who knew his address was threatened with extortion, that person would want to abandon his own apartment and stay with him and thus become a burden. It was said that one Jew looked like a Czech, but three Jews/Czechs—*trzech mężczyzn*—were immediately noticed.[1] Even a brother would not reveal his address to his own brother or a father to his son. But I was careless in this regard and wherever or whenever I could, I helped people as much as possible. It was in my nature to place my life and the lives of my wife and child in danger. At least twenty people would come to my place and knew my address. Among them was a professor from the University of Göttingen by the name of Alex Weichberg.

When Hitler came to power the Nazis dismissed thirty Jewish academicians from that university. Weichberg went to Russia. He was a genius in physics and mathematics. Later on, he married a Polish movie actress and changed his name to Zybilsky. He also gained fame as an author and wrote about his experiences in a book called *Die Hexenkessler*.[2] I had the book but someone took it from me, and I do not remember the editor. It is a fantastic book. Weichberg-Zybilsky, being a famous professor, had a leading position in Russia. He was Austrian

---

1 *Trzech mężczyzn* is Polish for "three men." This is a play on words, as the word *trzech* is pronounced like Czech, referring to someone from Czechoslovakia.
2 We could not find any information about the author or the book.

by birth. Hitler made a pact with Stalin whereby Russia would turn over all Germans to Germany. Since Austria had been incorporated into Germany, all Germans, as well as Austrians, were gathered and sent to Germany. This included Weichberg. He managed to escape somewhere in Germany. He told me the story, which is also in his book. Unfortunately, Weichberg is no longer alive. He survived the war and died in Paris or London. After the war he became a builder of entire blocks of houses.[3]

A judge by the name of Dr. Juliusz Mertz also used to come to my place. He had been the only Jewish judge in Tarnów; aside from him, one can state that the judicial system was *Judenrein*. I do not remember what name he used in Warsaw. He had contacts with the underground organization and obtained identification papers for people. He would get money from England, which he distributed to those in need. I have to recount his tragic death, because it is important.[4]

There was a woman, a certain Jadżka Bramowicz who was a light blond artist. She arrived in Warsaw with a little boy. She was originally from Kraków. She too used to come up to see us without the child. The child was always dressed as a little girl with long hair, yet he was a circumcised boy. Anyway, Juliusz Mertz and Jadżka Bramowicz, as well a few others—women and men—used to meet at a bakery on Mokotowska Street, which was not far from us. They met once or twice a week at the bakery where they would eat, drink, and talk. One day, Jadżka Bramowicz came to the bakery crying and wanting to make a phone call to the underground organization—actually, to Juliusz Mertz, who had a phone. She had no access to a telephone, so she came running to the bakery in tears. She called Juliusz Mertz; whether she reached him or not I do not know. The owner of the bakery, a Polish woman who knew Jadżka as a good customer, asked her why she was crying. Jadżka said the Gestapo raided her apartment where she lived and took her child. I later found out what happened. The owner of her apartment apparently was sewing uniforms of SS and other high officers for members of the underground organization, who would dress up as SS and other officials in order to stage acts of sabotage. The mother

3 Probably in England or France.
4 Powerful statement: in essence Dad feels that it is his responsibility to let people know about it.

had hidden the child inside her bed under covers. The child was getting air by turning toward the wall. I myself used to lay that way and, when a neighbor knocked on the door, my wife would hide me under the covers. Anyway, there was a raid on the apartment. I don't know whether it was successful or not, but that is not important now. As the Germans were leaving the apartment after the search, one of them got the idea to lift the bedcover, and he saw the hidden child. Though the child was in a dress, they were experts in such matters and discovered that it was a boy and that he was circumcised. They took the boy with them.

Jadżka Bramowicz, weeping, recounted the story to the bakery owner and said she did not know what to do. The bakery owner calmed her down and said: "Listen, I can help you. I have a friend who is a police officer here in Warsaw. He has connections and he will find the child and bring him back. Of course this will cost money." It was a rather large sum, though I don't remember the exact amount. Jadżka did not have any money, but she had contact with Juliusz Mertz, who always distributed three thousand *złotys* per person to Jews who lived as Aryans or were hiding with Aryans or to those who were without means. In any case, Mertz distributed quite a bit of money. Jadżka first sought assurances from the baker that for that sum her acquaintance, the police commissioner, would find the child. The money was collected among the Jews living underground as Aryans to save the child. I too gave a few thousand *złotys*. Jadżka went back to the bakery and said to the owner, "Listen well. I have contact to the underground organization and should this be a trap, I point out to you that the following day your shop will be blown up, and you will be dead."

"But what are you thinking? I only want to help," the owner replied. Finally, they agreed to meet in a park at a certain hour. A courier would come with the money, and the police captain would bring the child. Jadżka Bramowicz disappeared. It was a setup, and she was never seen again. Juliusz Mertz probably came on the usual day or hour to the pastry shop. He knew nothing about this, and he too disappeared from the surface of the earth.

Among the people who came to my place was a certain Irka Szalit, a girl who was friends with the two sisters. Before Juliusz Mertz disappeared, my wife had given him a photograph of herself so he could obtain a work permit for her in case she wanted to go out. There were roundups of young women and men to be sent to Germany to work. These people were just grabbed. My wife gave Juliusz Mertz a photo, as well as other information, including her name, Zofia Ślusarczyk, date of birth, and her address, which was Szucha 11. Irka Szalit was a friend of Juliusz Mertz and when he disappeared, she came to us and said, "You have to get out of the apartment." She knew that we had given Juliusz the photo and other information to get the work permit, and we knew that his apartment would be searched. We did not know if he had already submitted the photo or whether he still had it with him. So we dressed with great haste and fled the apartment. We had a reserve apartment on Czackiego Street. People always had a backup apartment, so as not to be stranded with a child without a roof over their heads.

But in the meantime, the following happened. Wanda Simcha, the lawyer, and her sister Riwka Simcha and her boyfriend, Rysiek Steiger, had their apartment raided by hoodlums who had found out that they were Jewish. They were beaten up and robbed of all their possessions. I have already told the story of Wanda having borrowed my wife's wedding ring, because she wanted to go to the gynecologist and was ashamed of not being a virgin and that the ring was taken away from her. So, they all came to us. It was winter; I cannot tell you whether it was December or January. We took them in, and the young man, who was about twenty years old and a light blond, slept on the floor. Incidentally, his father was a dentist and my brother-in-law was his assistant who worked as a dental technician. His father, Dr. Julek Steiger, was one of the most prominent members of our town. They came to us and said that Rysiek had nowhere to live. The two sisters could go anywhere, but Rysiek could not because he was covered with bruises and was bloodied. Therefore, the sisters Wanda and Riwka could not be seen with the young man. They knew my address and had no other choice but to come to us. The young man stayed with us for about one week or longer. My wife took out his excrements in a night pot, saying it was from her child. But this was too dangerous. I told Wanda Simcha and Rysiek, "Listen, I have a room, a backup room on Czackiego Street, but you must find a place somewhere else to place him. This room is for my security. I will give it to him for a few days since this is an emergency."

Everyone who had the resources insured himself with a backup place, in case he was blackmailed and if with *mazal* ("luck" in Hebrew) he was not delivered to the Gestapo. That was when one needed such a backup apartment, so as not to wind up living under the sky or under a bridge. As soon as Irka Szhalit, my wife's friend, notified us of Juliusz Mertz's disappearance, we fled the apartment and landed on Czackiego Street. We were scared that the Gestapo had already found the papers of the work permit with the address and the picture of my wife. We arrived at the room but it was locked. I did not have a second key. It was a room between two stories, like half a floor. So we stood and stood and stood, and it was getting late. The curfew hour rang, and we were standing on the street. We had no alternative but to go back home and wait for the Gestapo; to wait to see whether the Gestapo would or would not come; to wait to see if we would be lucky or not. Later, I found out that Irka Szhalit also had notified Wanda Simcha and Rysiek Steiger of Juliusz Mertz's disappearance, and they ran off with the key. We had no other choice but to go back to our apartment. We had no other backup, and we did not know any addresses anywhere among the Jewish Aryans. People knew my address, but I did not know a single one, because they kept it a secret. Thank God the Gestapo did not come for us.

The hunt for Jews was pursued not only by the Gestapo, but was instigated and exploited by the Poles themselves. They made a profession of it. There was a rumor going around that if you caught a Jew you would not have to work for the rest of your life, because they all believed that the Jews were all bankers. In fact, however, there was great poverty among the Jewish population in Poland. There were only a small number of Jews among the industrialists and other such positions. Out of a Jewish population of 3 million or 3.5 million there might have been perhaps 1 percent who were well off, who were wealthy. Perhaps 5 percent were part of the middle class.

One day a man, a certain Mr. Fessel, came up to us and said that there was a possibility of getting to Hungary. He had contact with a smuggler who knew the way through Czechoslovakia into Hungary and could smuggle people into

Hungary. There were rumors that in Hungary the Jews were untouched, that they lived a free life, that they were not being deported. No harm was done to the Jews in Hungary, it was said. The sisters, Natalka and Helenka, decided to go with their friend Klara, the engineer. But the two girls did not have the financial means, since you had to pay a certain sum per person for being smuggled across. There was a certain pervasive atmosphere among Jews about going. Even my wife said we should also go. As I have said and previously emphasized, I always acted according to my logic. I said to my wife that the trip and the illegal passage across the border had a 60–70 percent risk that we would perish. Here, at the present time, our apartment was not yet compromised,[5] meaning that it had not been revealed. I believed that as long as we still had a roof over our heads, I did not want to put myself in danger with my wife and the child by illegally crossing the border. But there was such an illusion, a myth, a mass delusion. It was rumored that this person was going and that person was going, so that my wife harassed me to go. In order to get her off my back, I said that I did not have the means to go. I did have the means, yet I told her that I had no money. She, however, did not believe me.

After I arrived in Warsaw, I also helped the friends I still had among the two hundred people who had been left behind in the Tarnów ghetto—the cleaning crew. There was a man named Kuba Hier, whom I mentioned earlier. He had not socialized with Jews, having completely assimilated. He used to associate mainly with judges and lawyers. He was from Drąbrowa, which was about sixty kilometers from Tarnów where he was the director of a savings and loan. He would come to Tarnów, our town, in a two-wheeled horse carriage, meet his people in a coffee shop, and ride back. Well, I want to tell you, he was like a prince or a baron. Kuba Hier later gave all his jewelry, which included a diamond ring, a gold watch on a chain, and a golden cigarette case among others items, to a friend of his, a lawyer, for safe keeping, since all Jews had to turn in all jewelry and gold to the *Bank Polski* (Polish Bank), essentially to the Germans. Kuba was a proper person and was afraid of doing anything illegal; he gave his jewelry to a trusted hand. I do not remember the lawyer's name.

---

5 Dad uses term *treif*, Yiddish for "not kosher."

Meanwhile, the lawyer, who was a Pole, was taken hostage and disappeared. Kuba Hier was left without any means of livelihood. He had been given an honorary job at the Jewish Council in the ghetto as a distributor of apartments and in charge of cataloguing the Jewish population in the ghetto. He was the director of this department. Kuba Hier had a female friend, Franciska or Franka Holzer, whose husband was a lawyer who had been taken hostage soon after the German occupation. Wherever the Germans came, they right away took hostages from among the elite, such as lawyers, doctors, and judges, and sent them off somewhere. Then there was another lawyer from Lemberg, a Dr. Korngold, with whom I became friends in the ghetto. I was, so to speak, the "capitalist" while still in the Tarnów ghetto. Franka Holzer worked at the laundry of the Jewish Council. Neither Dolek Korngold, the lawyer from Lemberg, nor Kuba Hier, the director of a savings and loan, nor Franka Holzer had the means to sustain themselves, and so, I gave them money.

Franka cooked in the laundry area and made bacchanalian-like meals,[6] though limited in amount. The Holzers once had an employee at their flour mill, who later became a cook at a passenger boat. He sent her recipes for the finest meals. She cooked with love. We lived close together due to the circumstances. We told Kuba Hier that the meals only cost a few *złotys*, though they cost many times that amount. But he did not have the means, as he was not getting any money from the Jewish Council. Dolek Korngold was deported during the ghetto liquidation. Only Kuba Hier and Franka Holzer remained. They knew that I was going away on Aryan papers, and they wanted me to send them papers, Aryan papers. When I met Juliusz Mertz in Warsaw, I gave him the necessary information, and he managed to obtain ID cards for them, which I sent to them to the ghetto with a female courier. Her name was Janka. She was able to bring Franka Holzer to Warsaw. Kuba Hier, however, was supposedly sent somewhere to Siberia and as soon as he arrived there, he was shot in the neck and killed. His ID card was therefore useless.

As noted, Franka Holzer—Steir was her maiden name—came to Warsaw from the ghetto in Tarnów. She had a 100 percent Jewish appearance—a nose

---

6 Original term used by Dad.

like the one shown in the *Stürmer* (Nazi propaganda newspaper) and black hair—but she had a figure like Venus de Milo, though this is now unimportant. She did not have an apartment, so Janka brought her to me. The two young sisters still lived with us as well, in addition to the three of us, so that she had to sleep on the floor. We put something under her and covered her. Because of her "Jewish" face, it was impossible for Franka Holzer to live as an Aryan. Stefan Klara managed to find a place for her, which was sublet from a *Volksdeutsche* or Polish woman, with the help of the underground organization. The woman's husband was in the SS or a soldier, I don't know for sure. In any case, she agreed that Franka could stay with her and that she would feed her for three thousand or four thousand *złotys*. Since her husband was on the front, the woman took her in and Franka was brought to her. One day during winter, Franka Holzer came back to us. "What happened?" we asked. A colleague of the landlady's husband, supposedly an SS man, visited her. He was on leave and her husband had given the SS man the address of his wife and told him he could stay with her. He had a few days' leave, so that Franka had to get out of there during that time, since the landlady was scared that he would discover her. The landlady had hidden Franka in a kind of pantry and when the SS man went out, Franka was told to disappear for a few days until he left. So she landed with us again.

In addition to being friends with Zigmund Hollender, I was also friends with Haskel Hollender, the father of Zigmund. When I had told Haskel that I was leaving the ghetto for Warsaw he said to me, "Tell Zigmund to arrange an apartment for me, since I am leaving for Warsaw any day now." Zigmund Hollender and his wife used to come up to our room. He would always warn me when not to go out, as noted earlier. One day I was at Zigmund Hollender's place and said to him: "Zigmund, you should know that your father told me that you are supposed to get him an apartment." He answered me: "That is my father; let that not be your concern.[7] I will take care of it, because he is my father." And one day, Marian Urban, my messenger, brought Haskel Hollender to me from the Tarnów ghetto. The son was notified. He came and said that he could not risk

---

7   "*Zerbreche Dir nicht den Kopf*"; German/Yiddish expression; literal translation: "Don't break your head."

having his apartment burned[8] by taking his father in, though Haskel Hollender wore a mustache like a Polish landowner and spoke a good Polish. He spoke no Yiddish and was from the "high-life" of our town. He was in construction and manufactured pipes for canals. He also had his own house with carpets. Marian Urban brought him to me. And this old man, who was at least thirty years older than me, slept on the floor. We were close friends. I had helped him when he came from Lemberg to Tarnów and did not have any financial means. His forests and factories had been confiscated, whereas I still had jewelry and had the means. He had said to me: "Schlomek, give me something to sell."[9] Initially I had loaned him about ten thousand or twenty thousand *złotys* and he said, "I owe you; I want to work, I can sell something, I can earn some money. Give me something to sell." Even though I did not need to sell anything, I gave him the possibility to earn some money. That is how he fed himself in Tarnów. He had a wife and a grandson, who by the way was paralyzed. His parents, a lawyer and his wife, had been deported. So Haskel Hollender stayed with us in Warsaw for about a week until one day his son came and said that he had an apartment for his father, namely a small guesthouse on Theater Place, number 5. I said to Zigmund: "You are crazy; guesthouses and hotels are watched during wartime." "This is only temporary," he responded. He would take care of it and nothing would happen to his father. He was taking big chances. He was 100 percent reckless toward his father, yet not toward himself. God forbid he should take his father into his apartment. He was afraid that the owner of the apartment or the neighbors might compromise his apartment.

---

8 "Burned" is a term used by hidden Jews to indicate that the apartment had been compromised, thus had to be vacated.
9 Presumably on commission.

📑 Historical Notes

Undisclosed addresses. Historian Gunnar S. Paulson corroborates Father's account that "addresses, for all those living in hiding, were a matter of the utmost secrecy, Jews on the Aryan side have to act like real conspirators. No one knows their addresses. One brother does not know the address of the other; children do not know the addresses of their parents." *Secret City: The Hidden Jews of Warsaw, 1940–1945* (New Haven, CT: Yale University Press, 2002), 101.

Meeting places. As surprising as it might be, Jews met openly in cafés. Diane Ackerman mentions two such cafés in Warsaw in her book *The Zookeeper's Wife* (New York: Norton, 2007).

18

Franka Holzer

One evening I went out to take care of something. Of course I was wearing my uniform. Nobody was at home except for Franka Holzer and my wife and child. It was winter. I came back taking the streetcar and Franka Holzer was not there. "Where is Franka?" I knew that she trembled with fear and that she would not go out alone for any money in the world. My wife told me that engineer Stefan Klara had taken her to Haskel Hollender at the Theater Place by a rickshaw. I asked, "Who authorized that?" My wife told me that the two young women, the two sisters, wanted it. They said that Franka was a danger to them, and besides they said I had brought a girlfriend home. The two girls had incited my wife into believing that Franka was my girlfriend; that I slept with her; that I had brought my girlfriend straight into the one room where two women and my wife lived. I was extremely angry. I said to the girls, "This is my apartment; I bought it with my money. What right do you have to throw her out?"

I had been at Haskel Hollender's place once, so I knew his address. It was Saturday. I went out on the street and called Haskel Hollender at the guesthouse. "I want to speak to Mr. Kowalski," which was his Aryan name, or something like. A child's voice answered saying that Mr. Kowalski was not there. "And Mrs. Janicka?" which was Franka's Aryan name. "She is also not here." So I thought that she had gone out to have her hair dyed blond, since her Jewish appearance plus her black hair scared her. She was scared and probably went to a hairdresser, I thought, and did not want to go alone and therefore took Hollender along. Then, I thought to myself, Haskel lived in a guesthouse; he got his lunches there, since he did not dare to go out unless he had to. We all knew of the many blackmailings taking place. It happened to Zigmund Hollender, even though he looked like a gentile. In fact, when I first saw him, I trembled, thinking he was a blackmailer. So, I figured that at one o'clock Haskel should be home. I went there at one and rang the doorbell. The apartment was on the second floor. A little girl, about eight or nine years of age, opened the door just a tiny bit. "Is Mr. Kowalski here?" I asked. "No." "And Mrs. Janicka?" "Not here either." So I shoved her aside. I knew that the first door to the right was Kowalski's. I opened the door, went in, and saw right away that a tragedy had happened here. The bed linen was on the floor. I saw his briefcase, containing pictures that were all torn up. I saw that they had been taken that night. I asked the girl, "What happened?" "Last night, the Gestapo and police came and they took them; they also took my parents." She was all alone in the guesthouse, which had about five or six rooms. Now I got goose bumps; maybe the Gestapo had the house under observation, checking everybody who entered. It was common procedure with the Gestapo that, when they discovered a nest, they would place two secret agents to see who came in and they would stop him, check his papers to see if he belonged to any of the underground organizations.

I had goose bumps as I stepped out of the building in my railroader's uniform. I did not want to turn around too often or they might think that I was scared. I walked in the direction of the streetcar and turned the corner. Then I turned around, but no one was there. The first thing I did when I got home, half dead, was to deliver the news that Hollender was gone and that Franka Holzer was gone. I got very angry at the young women, calling them murderesses. There was a sense of rage, and I have not talked to the two young women since. I called them murderesses. I had been able to save a woman; I got her out of the ghetto. And as for the two young women, I had endangered my life, had bought them fur coats, had arranged for the two railroaders to take them to Warsaw, only to have them act in such a reprehensible way to me and of course to Franka Holzer. I visited Franka's brother in Haifa after the war and gave him the news. Franka Holzer had told me she had a brother in Palestine and had asked me that, should I survive, I should give him greetings from her. I have not talked to these two women since then.

Then, the issue of leaving for Hungary started to heat up again. One day while sitting at the table I heard the two sisters talking. The older one, Natalka Hubler, said, "If he will pay you for the room, that's fine, and if not, place an ad in the paper. There will be hundreds of people coming and you can get at least thirty thousand or forty thousand *złotys* for it." I did not realize right away what room they were talking about. I had not talked to them for a week, because I really considered them murderesses. Then she repeated: "You can get a very good price." That is when I realized that they wanted to sell the apartment where I lived with my wife and child and which I had bought with my money. So, I approached them and asked, "What apartment are you talking about?" Natalka answered, "This apartment." I said, "How come? I bought this apartment for my wife with my money and paid for it. What right do you have to sell it?"

"The apartment is in my name." My wife had told the younger sister that she could register the apartment in her name. "That is bottomless malice; that is criminal. It is not enough that you have a murder on your conscience, the murder of Franka Holzer. And more so, I saved your lives, put my life in jeopardy, and got you the fur coats." The older sister said in front of her sister and my wife, "You slept with my sister; you did not do this for nothing." I said, "Helenka, you have nothing to say?" She lowered her eyes and did not say a word. I want to show you how life was then; people walked on corpses. I said, "Listen, I swear I will not give you a penny. This is pure blackmail, and besides, if you place an ad in the paper, the people coming to see the apartment will know that we are Jewish." It was not only the issue of the apartment. Any potential renter who saw my face, the face of my wife and of the child, would know we are Jewish; he would notice. I said, "Then I will take a hatchet and chop your head off!" I was exceedingly upset and angry. Without any doubt that was the most despicable behavior I had ever encountered. First, she said that I had brought a girlfriend home with me; then she accused me of having slept with her sister and that I did nothing for nothing. I had never had the "pleasure" of being alone in a room with her. There was a real commotion. My wife knelt in front of me, kissing my hands and pleading, "Give it to her." "Absolutely not," I said.

Alex Weichberg-Zybilsky, the professor from Göttingen, came up to (see) us. I said to him, "Mr. Alex, these two women want to blackmail me. You have some influence, don't you?" I don't know how they knew each other. He said, "Please, I do not want to interfere in this matter." And he left, realizing the tense atmosphere. Then, Stefan Klara came up to us and I said, "Mr. Klara, I need to talk to you." "Sure." He sat down, and I said, "Your friend and her sister want to blackmail me. They are blackmailing me to pay them for my apartment or otherwise they threaten to sell it. You have some influence with them. I will not give them one złoty, because this is blackmail. Besides, they owe their lives to me." He answered me: "Mr. Andrzej, I want the women to have as much money as possible, and I do not want to know how they get it." I told him, "Thank you for listening to me. I will keep my opinion about your character and your reply to myself. Thank you." Incidentally, he is no longer alive. And then my wife started to kiss my hands, pleading I should give them money, so that we should not be left homeless.

I finally gave them twenty thousand *złotys*, to make sure that they left. I am ashamed to say this now. First of all, I swore that if I survived and if they survived, the first thing I would do is slap their faces in public and spit in their faces. These two ladies had been raised in affluence and came from a decent family, and yet they behaved so despicably, both toward my wife and toward Franka Holzer. And they left for Hungary along with Stefan Klara. A whole group took the train. We had some heart palpitations fearing that if they were caught, questioned, and tortured by the Gestapo, they would reveal where they had lived in Warsaw, and the Gestapo would come to get us. So I did not know whether I should pray for them to be caught, just out of my rage for being such bad people, or whether I should pray that they got through without incident. In fact, they landed somewhere not too far from the border with Yugoslavia, when the train was stopped. They came out of the train and there was a whole gang of Gestapos and police waiting. They took them all away. Only Stefan Klara and one of the Alexandrowitzes from Kraków were saved, because they did not come out of the train, and in the meantime, the train resumed its journey. This is like a movie running in my head, but it's been thirty-nine or forty years since these events.

So we learned that the entire group was doomed. There were people known to be smugglers, who were also employed as spies, and they turned the group in. We found out after the war that the two sisters and the entire group were taken to Plaszów near Kraków. Natalka Hubler became a pianist in the orchestra of *Obersturmbandführer* Göth, the camp leader at Plaszów, and she survived the war. I found that out after the war. I visited Warsaw after the war, when Poland was under Russian occupation, under the Communists. I went to a coffee shop where the big shots of the government used to congregate. And there appeared a lady with a silver fox and threw her arms around my neck. I neither spat in her face, nor did I slap her. On one hand I was glad she had survived, and on the other I felt a deep rage. Anyway, I just could not hit her. I guess that is my nature. Well, that is the story.

🗐 Historical Notes

The importance of blending in. On pages 220–222 of her book *The Zoo-keeper's Wife* (New York: Norton, 2007), Diane Ackerman, describes in great detail various ways Poles helped Jews blend into the native population. She writes about the "cosmetic tricks to disguise Jews, with some salons specializing in more elaborate ruses. … Jewish women [were given] lessons on how to appear Aryan … [were taught] Christian prayers, how to behave in church and at ceremonial events." Knowing how to cook and serve pork, prepare traditional Polish dishes, and order moonshine vodka could be of high importance. "Typically, when the police stopped Jews on the street, they checked the men for circumcision and ordered the women to recite the Lord's Prayer and Hail Mary," Ackerman writes. A "Semitic" nose also had to be camouflaged. Some Polish surgeons provided surgical means to alter noses and restore foreskins.

Hairstyles and hair color were another worry for Jews. Black hair was often bleached to just the right shade, not too pale and not too dark. According to Ackerman, "Aryan hairstyles banned bangs, curls, or frizz." I remember Mother telling me that there was a "conference" at one time over whether to bleach my very black hair. It was decided not to do so because Mother's hair was black and it would look suspicious to have a blond daughter. However, Mother was advised not to take me to the market with her as I looked "too Jewish." Although Mother's hair was also black, her fine features gave her more of an Italian than Jewish appearance.

19

The Righteous Pharmacist

I mentioned earlier that Judge Juliusz Mertz had money to distribute for charitable Jewish causes through the underground organization. I told you before how I saw through a window as my good friends from Tarnów, Eddie and Estera Blumenkrantz, were being led away during the liquidation of the ghetto in Tarnów. Estera had given her child and the child's grandmother for hiding to a pharmacist in Tarnów, a certain Jadwiga (sometime before the final liquidation). The name of the grandmother was Liluska Rosenblut and the name of the girl was Leah. The pharmacist in turn gave the child to a cloister for hiding. Jadwiga also accommodated Mrs. Rosenblut, the grandmother of the child, somewhere in a village close by a river named Czarny Dunajec.[1] I knew that there was nobody left to take care of the girl and the grandmother since the parents had been deported. Jadwiga was employed by the health department as a pharmacist, and I assumed she could not afford to support the grandmother. Her first name was Jadwiga and she married a certain Filozow. By the way, my wife still corresponds with Leah (in 1981). I knew her father, who used to be a client of mine. He used to buy watches and other gift items from me. He was of modest means, working as a mechanic for the railroad. I did not sleep at nights, worrying whether perhaps the grandmother had no money and therefore no means to live. I made contact with a messenger; I forget his name now. He was a *Volksdeutsche* who lived in Kraków. I told him: "Listen, please drive to

---

1   Dad calls it Czarny Donai, which means Black Donai, and it is not clear if this is the name of the village or the river. Felicia found a river by the name of Dunajec and a town by the name of Czarny Dunajec on the Polish-Slovakian border about sixty kilometers south of Kraków.

Tarnów. I'll pay you the traveling costs plus two thousand *złotys*" or some sum like that, for his efforts. "Drive to the pharmacy of the health department" on this and that street. "There works a certain Mrs. Filozowa. Tell her you want to talk to her in private and inquire if she is in need of money. Give her my best regards, using my real name, so to speak my "real" name.[2] Tell her that I sent you to inquire if the grandmother, Mrs. Rosenblut, is alive and if she needs money." Judge Juliusz Mertz, as noted earlier, had money for Jewish charitable causes from the underground, and I planned to obtain some money for her. The messenger should also inquire how the child was doing. I told the messenger to report to me personally, as the postal service was not much in use.

Two days went by and the man arrived and told me the following: At first Mrs. Filozowa said she knew no one by the name of Lederberger or Mrs. Rosenblut, and that he should stop bothering her, and that she had no time for him. I had prepared the messenger that she would deny everything since she would be frightened that her life would be in danger. However, he was able to convince her that this was the *emes*, the pure truth, and then she started to cry. She told him that she had to pawn her fur coat and that she no longer had the means to support the old Mrs. Rosenblut, who herself had no money. The child had been accommodated in a cloister and did not require any money, but she, Mrs. Filozowa, urgently needed money and urged the messenger to get back to me. Since the messenger did not yet have the opportunity to talk to Juliusz Mertz, I gave the messenger all the money I had in my possession, about ten thousand or over ten thousand *złotys*. I gave him the money, and he went back to her and she received the money. The messenger was a highly trustworthy and wonderful man.

In the meantime, the tragedy with Juliusz Mertz took place when he disappeared after going to the bakery, so that I never received the money back from him. I still had jewelry, but did not want to go to stores to sell them, but instead gave the jewelry to Mr. Hirsh to sell it for dollars. And that is what he did so that I had a few hundred dollars, which was a lot of money during wartime, as the dollar was very strong. And from that I lived until the uprising, the Polish Warsaw uprising (of August 1944.)

---

2 Dad is referring to his original name—Salomon Lederberger.

20

The Warsaw Uprising

Now I want to paint a different picture: There was talk that the Russians and Americans were making progress. Even in Warsaw the Germanic "strong men," the soldiers, ran away. They retreated not in an organized manner the way they had marched in, but were seen dragging their boots, just like the Polish army had looked during their retreat. And the Polish people, myself included, stood there and yelled at the retreating soldiers and threw rotten eggs and spoiled potatoes at them. The Germans did not respond but marched toward the west, toward the homeland. We found out that the Russians were at the Vistula River. They were in Praga, a suburb of Warsaw, which is across the river from Warsaw (on the right bank of the Vistula River). The German civilians had already been evacuated. When the Polish underground, the AK (*Armia Krajowa*—Home Army) and AL (*Armia Ludowa*—People's Army), saw the retreat of German troops and the evacuation of German civilian employees, they started an uprising in order to prevent the Germans from devastating Warsaw. We were glad to see the Germans retreat, but the Russians remained pat in Praga by Warsaw for six months. They stayed there without firing a single bullet. When Hitler and his regime saw that the Russians did not move, Hitler gave the order to level the city to soot and ashes. The Polish resistance counted on the fact that the Russians were only a few kilometers away. But what actually happened? The Russian army did not cross the Vistula, but instead just stayed put and waited, smoked cigarettes, drank vodka, and did not fire one shot. So, what did those gangsters, the Nazis, do? They organized different groups of gangsters—a certain Dirlewanger comes to mind—and sent a reprisal expedition to Warsaw to mow down the uprising and burn out the entire population; to get the Polish population moving out and going west. They wanted to subdue the people. They blew up entire blocks of houses. They used entire battalions of flame-throwers using explosives experts. They used airplanes to quell the uprising of the Poles who had no tanks, no other means of defense, only an occasional revolver or hand grenade, which the Polish resistance had obtained by raiding military depots. The Polish resistance was not successful against the overwhelming German might, and many were murdered.

🗐 Historical Notes

The Warsaw Uprising. Encyclopedia Britannica, under "Warsaw Uprising (August–October 1944)," describes the unsuccessful Polish attempt to seize control of Warsaw before the Russians. Although "Soviet authorities encouraged Polish underground to start the revolt which began August 1, 1944 . . . the Red Army, which occupied a suburb across the Vistula River from Warsaw, remained idle, and the Soviet government refused to allow the western Allies to use Soviet air bases to airlift supplies to the Poles." The Polish underground forces surrendered October 2, 1944. *Encyclopedia Britannica, Deluxe Edition* (Chicago: Encyclopedia Britannica, 2010).

The **Dirlewanger** Father mentions, refers to Dr. Oskar Dirlewanger (26 September 1895—7 June 1945). According to the Holocaust Research Project, he was a World War II officer of the SS who commanded the SS-Sturmbrigade *Dirlewanger*, a penal battalion composed of German criminals and valued for its particular brutality.

> "His unit was also active in the suppression of the Polish uprising in Warsaw which commenced in August 1944 … On 5 August Dirlewanger's SS barbarians advanced about 1,000 yards – in every single street in the Wola district of Warsaw … [T]he inhabitants were ordered to leave their homes, induced by promises of evacuation. As soon as large groups of civilians assembled on the streets, they were not taken to evacuation points but were herded together in cemeteries, gardens, back yards, factory forecourts or squares, soldiers then fired machine gun bursts into the human mass until there were no further signs of movement … [T]he soldiers piled the corpses in large heaps, poured petrol over them and set them on fire. Hospitals in the Wola and Ochota areas suffered worst of all that day. The "good fellows" as Himmler called them, with Dirlewanger at their head, stormed into the wards, shot the sick and wounded where they lay. Nurses, nuns, helpers and doctors suffered the same fate. Dirlewanger received his final promotion,

to *SS-Oberfuehrer der Reserve*, on August 15th 1944 and for his actions in the Warsaw uprising he was awarded the Knights Cross on September 30, 1944. In May 1945 Dirlewanger's men were taken into Soviet captivity but he fled westwards and was arrested in Altshausen. Dirlewanger died on 7 June 1945, killed either by soldiers or former concentration camp inmates, the exact details are unknown."

http://www.holocaustresearchproject.org/einsatz/dirlewanger.html

21

Flight from Warsaw

We lived in an area with villas, which had front yards and gardens in the back. We heard the shooting, but there was no activity in our area; these occurred in other parts of the city. We sat around and waited for help from heaven. One day, German soldiers came in a row moving through our garden, cutting through the fences in order to send us away. Soldiers told me, "Give me all your gold and jewelry, since it will be taken away from you anyway by General Vlassov of the Ukrainians; they will take all your valuables and perhaps maybe also your life." I said that I had nothing to give and they sent us going westward. That was October 1944. It was a very hot day, and the houses on both sides of the street were burning. We hid our most precious possessions that we could not take with us in the basement inside a container. We took two suitcases with the most important things, such as a suit, shirts, and personal belongings for the child. And so we marched westward. We saw people carrying their belongings. It was more than a few kilometers to the west. Everywhere suitcases were left behind filled with whatever you can imagine, such as silverware and fur coats, since it was impossible to march carrying such belongings. If somebody happened to have a bicycle, he loaded up things on it only to see the bicycle taken away and the belongings thrown away by soldiers. I wore my uniform hat and was dressed as a railroader. Most likely, however, the railroaders had also organized themselves in an underground organization. They (the German soldiers) yelled at us: "You were shooting at us, you gangster." So I threw away my uniform jacket and my hat. They kept on searching me for weapons and took my razor blade away. Whatever they found on me, they took.

🗐 Historical Notes

Andrey Andreyevich Vlasov or Vlassov September 14, 1900 – August 2, 1946) was a Russian Red Army general who collaborated with Nazi Germany during World War II. In his book *The Rising '44: The Battle for Warsaw*, Norman Davies wrote that there are two major misunderstandings on the matter of General Vlasssov's participation in the Warsaw Uprising. "It is often said that the collaborationist forces in Warsaw included 'Vlassovites' and also Ukrainians from the 14th *Waffen-SS Galizien* Division …Vlassov was not in Warsaw. Indeed the Vlassov Army was not formally constituted until the winter of 1944-45 … The source of the mistake seems to derive from the fact that part of the RONA Brigade" which took part in the uprising, was broken up after the Rising and transferred to the Vlassov Army. *The Rising '44: The Battle for Warsaw*, (New York: Penguin, 2003), pages 284–286

Polish Home Army. On October 3, 1944, the BBC News reported that the Polish Home Army and the citizens of Warsaw rose up against the Germans … During the uprising more than 15,000 rebels were killed and up to a quarter of the city's one million inhabitants slaughtered. After the city was crushed, the Germans ordered all the inhabitants to leave and systematically razed the city. The Red Army entered Warsaw in January 1945, and the Soviet Union formally recognized the Communist Lublin Committee as the provisional Polish government. It suited Stalin to see the Polish Home Army, who owed allegiance to the Polish government in exile in London and not to Lublin, destroyed by the Germans. … By March, the whole of pre-war Poland was occupied by the Soviet army. BBC, "1944: Poles Surrender After Warsaw Uprising," On This Day, BBC News website, http://news.bbc.co.uk/onthisday/hi/dates/stories/october/3/newsid_3560000/3560811.stm.

 # Transit Camp: Pruszków

And so we marched westward, a population of a million people, until we arrived to a huge area surrounded by fences. This was the Pruszków transit camp. It was also a repair station for locomotives and railroads. They put us in the camp. The young people were segregated to be sent to work in Germany. My wife and the child were moved somewhere else, and I was readied to be sent to work in Germany. A train stood by for the trip to Germany. There were thousands of people. I was in no hurry to board the train and waited each time until the train was fully loaded with no possibility to get on. There still remained a few thousand or perhaps tens of thousands of people who did not get on the trains. It turned night, and the last train departed. They ordered us to a barrack to get some sleep until the next morning when the next train would come and ship us to Germany. During the night we slept on concrete floors. There was no other alternative. I had thrown my luggage away when I became separated from my wife and child. I remember my wife gave me two pieces of sugar, a piece of soap, and a towel.[1] That was my "baggage"—only the most essential; no toothbrush, no toothpaste. So I kept on thinking all night how to get out of this mess. By the way, as the day broke, I went under a faucet where there was an outflow of water and I washed myself entirely with cold water and dried myself. I am quite hardened to cold water. Since people were still asleep, I took my time bathing, or rather washing myself from the heat of the day and the long march.

---

1 Note from Felicia: "I remember going between the women's side and the men's side a couple of times bringing these things to Dad. The last time I went, a German soldier told me that if I crossed to the men's side one more time, he would not allow me to return to my mother."

I started to think how to establish contact with my wife. I went to the entrance of the camp, which was a wide door, as it was a huge barrack. A guard stood there with a machine gun. I went to him and started to talk to him in purposefully very poor German. Anyway, I speak German poorly; it is more of a Yiddish. I spoke with a hard accent just as the Poles do. Warsaw had been under Russian rule during the First World War, when Poland was divided among Austria, Hungary, and Russia. Galicia belonged to Austria-Hungary; Warsaw and Lithuania belonged to Russia. Therefore the people of Warsaw did not speak German, their second language being Russian. In Galicia the second language was German. I personally never much studied the German language. I never was much of a student and had only completed middle school where we studied German only superficially. That was because the Poles hated the Germans; yet, one had to study a second language. I started to speak to the guard to inquire if he knew where the women and children were being accommodated. He said to me: "How come you know German?" I said: "I lived for a while in Oberschlesien, in Katowice," which had belonged to Poland, "so I learned a little German."

Then, I proceeded to tell him a fairy-tale: "Listen, please, my wife somehow got lost and during the separation I gave my four-year-old child to a strange woman, and I want to give this woman my address or take her address and her name. So please give me the opportunity to find her, as you are probably also a father." He appeared somewhat older, about forty or forty-five years old. The guard said, "Listen, indeed I am a father and I feel very sorry for you. The women and children are housed in the barracks over there, but listen to me, and do not go over there now." Those barracks were also guarded by a guard who walked back and forth. "When the guard moves back, crawl over, since I am responsible and am not allowed to let you out." Anyway, I succeeded to get into that barrack and everyone, women and children, were lying on the floor. Whoever had anything to lie on, did so.[2] Finally, I discovered my wife. She was in the company of Mrs. Dąbrowska, the teacher who had lived on the ground floor with her mother-in-law in Warsaw. I went to them. Every

---

2 Note from Felicia: "I vaguely remember lying on the cement floor, my head on the suitcase, being very cold. I trace my rheumatic pains in my right shoulder whenever the weather changes, from that event."

fifteen or twenty minutes the Germans walked around and searched for young people to drag them away. So what to do? Then the teacher said that she had a bandage. "Oh," I said, "very good." I bandaged my left hand and with the help of a towel, I hung my left arm, as if I had a broken hand. And, in fact, they came to me and saw the bandage and did not take me out. I remained with the women and children. Here and there other older men were seen in the barrack.

Another selection process then followed. A group of male and female physicians, all Polish except for the chief physician, of course, proceeded to examine people. In order to be exempt from working you had to declare yourself sick. They even took mothers who had children of ages six, seven, or eight. I don't know what they did with the children. They probably inducted them into the Hitler youth and sent the mothers to Germany to work. Our daughter was four years old—it was 1944—but she was small, like a two-year-old. Therefore, at the checkpoint my wife said that Felicia was two years old, since it was said that up to the age of two mothers along with their children were let go. And so, during the inspection and during the separation process, my wife said that her child was two years old, and they let her go outside the camp. I wound up in another barrack, where physicians examined people for *Seuchenkrankheit* (dysentery) and segregated the healthy ones, who were sent to work, from the old and sick ones, who were exempt from work. The Polish physicians and health-care workers were all dressed in white uniforms. In order to save young people from being sent to work, they diagnosed them with dysentery, whereas those, presumably older people, who actually had dysentery were not declared sick. Among the doctors was a very fine older Polish female physician. At least compared to me she was much older. It was 1944, and I was thirty-five years old—in other words in my best years. She said to me: "You have dysentery" or something similar. I said, "Good." "You have a contagious disease; you have dysentery." I asked: "What do I say when they ask me what my symptoms are?" "That you run to the toilet and that you have bloody bowel movements." So they declared me as having dysentery.

There were perhaps two hundred people, men and women in the room, all young and healthy. We were placed in a special barrack designated for those with dysentery. On the door was written: "Attention! Entrance Forbidden:

Dysentery." Then a female physician announced that we should all sit down and that we would shortly be moved to Tworki. Tworki was a well-known mental institution about forty to fifty kilometers from Warsaw. As you certainly know, as is known all over the world, the Germans took all the mentally ill, and anesthesiologists gassed them to death. That institution was apparently converted to a hospital for patients with dysentery. We were supposedly to be transported under the supervision of guards from our barrack to the exit of the camp, which was about one kilometer away. So our guards arrived to take us to Tworki, where we were to be under isolation. I walked at the front of the row and assumed the role of a translator for the guards. Whenever the guard said something in German and the group did not understand, I translated for them. As we arrived at the exit, the large gate opened widely, big enough to let a truck through. It was even wide enough to let trains pass through. Two cars with officers dressed in black uniforms, golden buttons, and golden chains came toward us. One of the officers asked the guard at the gate: "Where are they going? Where does this transport go to?" To which the guard who led the group answered: "These all are people with dysentery who are on their way to the hospital in Tworki." "Everybody back. It is full there; there is no more room," the officer yelled. So, we all went back to our barrack, which was under isolation. Everybody lay down on what looked like mattresses, because an inspection could come anytime. These so-called mattresses were made of wood shavings with cement in the shape of blocks, which looked like mattresses, but were probably used for building walls. There were plenty of these blocks. I sat down and we talked about what to do. Everybody had his own ideas, when a female physician, who was probably the physician-in-chief, and a Pole came running in and said that everybody should lie down as the inspectors were on their way. We should not stand around, should not talk, but lie down as if we were sick. So I lay down on this concrete block and after ten or fifteen minutes, a group of ten to fifteen inspectors came in. Among them was also a woman in uniform. They walked around, row by row, looked to the right and to the left. I was lying as if really sick. And imagine, this is really a unique situation; there were perhaps two hundred people and they stopped by me. I heard as one of them said: "This one seems to be an imposter," someone feigning illness. One guy approached me and took my pulse and looked at his watch and said, "No, he is really ill." Most likely, I had heart palpitations and my pulse was difficult to feel. They made only this one inspection and left. The lady physician, who had warned us of the arrival of the inspectors, came running in, telling me that I had saved her and the entire physician staff. I, a Jew, had saved them. Of all the two hundred people, and I am sure the only Jew, I was selected by the inspector, who said, "This one seems to be an imposter."[3] I have to tell you what a coincidence that was!

What incredible experiences we went through. Anyway, after the inspection, the inspectors probably drove away, and we were locked in the barrack. It became known that we were to go to Tworki after all. So, we all got up and again marched to the exit. When we arrived at the exit door, everybody ran away, some to the right, some to the left, and some straight ahead. And the guards did nothing. They neither shot at us nor took any other action. They were older people and did nothing. So, we took off. Now, where to go and how to get there? Where could I find my wife? I walked perhaps several kilometers in search of a village, which had to be somewhere, when I saw an electric train standing in the middle of nowhere. It was filled with people—women, men, and children. The train had come to a stop because the entire electricity went off. So the train was stuck in the middle of a field. Next to the train I discovered a kiosk, where they sold bread and cured meat. I bought a pound and a loaf of white bread, as I had not eaten for two or three days. Once the Red Cross had come by to the camp with soup, but one needed plates to get some. They also threw some bread at the hungry crowd, and I actually caught a piece of bread, but there were two elderly people, perhaps in their eighties. So I divided the bread and gave each one half, since for me it did not matter; I could go on hungry. Anyway, I took the bread into the tram and was about to sit down and to eventually eat my food. And there in the tram I discovered my wife.[4] Of course the joy was great. But now, where should we go? Where to? We had to somehow find accommodations in a village.

---

3 Dad is being sarcastic that he, a Jew among two hundred people, had saved the gentiles.
4 Dad is crying.

I had money, though I was constantly being searched. I also always had jewelry on me. They would frisk me, but I had a jeweler's pocket in the back of my pants, a special pocket, where I kept dollars and jewelry. It never occurred to them to look there. They only searched the pockets of my pants and my jacket. I therefore luckily succeeded in keeping everything.

🗐 Historical Notes

Deportation from Warsaw and the Pruszków camp. *In Memorial Book: The Transport of Poles from Warsaw to Concentration Camp Auschwitz, 1940–1945* [Ksiêga Pamiêci: Transporty Polaków z Warszawy do KL Auschwitz 1940–1945], Felicia found the following information about the deportation of Warsaw residents to Pruszków camp:

> In the course of the Warsaw Uprising and its suppression, the Germans deported approximately 550,000 of the city's residents and approximately 100,000 civilians from its outskirts, sending them to *Durchgangslager* 121 (*Dulag* 121), a transit camp in Pruszków set up especially for this purpose. The security police and the SS segregated the deportees and decided their fate. An estimated 650,000 people passed through the Pruszków camp in August, September, and October. About 55,000 were sent to concentration camps, including 13,000 to Auschwitz.

Kazimierz Albin, Franciszek Piper, and Irena Strzelecka, *Ksiêga Pamiêci: Transporty Polaków z Warszawy do KL Auschwitz 1940–1945*, Polish Edition (Oświęcimiem: Państwowe Muzeum Auschwitz-Birkenau, 2000), http://www.warsawuprising.com/paper/auschwitz_museum.htm.

On the World War II Museum website (http://www.ww2museums.com), Kaj Metz adds that a "couple of thousand people died in *Durchgangslager* 121 Prusków due to the terrible living conditions. The camp was closed in December 1944." Today only one of the original camp guard towers is still standing. On the wall in front of the tower is a sign that reads "Warsaw walked through here in the summer of 1944."

When Felicia visited the camp in 2005, the guide told the group that the large oak tree that stands in front of that wall was a "witness to the atrocities committed there." He himself was in that camp as a ten-year-old boy.

 **Life on the Farm**

We walked in the direction where we would be able to stay somewhere overnight. However, whenever we came to a farmhouse, they had no room. There were after all thousands of people on the go. There were about one million people forced to move westward from Warsaw by the Germans. Let's assume that they let one hundred thousand or two hundred thousand go, though there is no way I would know the exact number. We got to this one farm, but they too had no room and had turned away many people. They allowed us, however, to stay the night in the barn, where we slept on hay. We stayed overnight and moved on. We did not know the area, but we accidentally met a man from Tarnów, also a Jew, who was living on Aryan papers. His name was Pelek Perlberger. He was a lawyer. Pelek told me: "Listen, I know of a place." He lived somewhere with peasants and had also survived the Warsaw devastation. He looked like a 100 percent Aryan, with blond hair. He was young, perhaps two or three years older than I, but we knew each other well. He was a wonderful chess player and always won the first prize in tournaments. He led us to a farm in some village and said, "You will be able to get shelter there." Since my name was Andrzej Białecki and my wife's papers were on Zofia Ślusarczyk, we could hardly present ourselves as a married couple. So I became the "uncle" and the child called me "uncle." After all, the child had not seen me for a long time after she left the ghetto in Tarnów (from October 1942 to September 1943) and she was then only about two and a half years of age. She called me "uncle," believing that I was a friend of her father's whom I had promised to take care of his wife and child should anything happen to him. We went into the farmhouse and I negotiated with the peasant. He wanted three thousand *złotys* a month to live there. As I was "not her husband," my wife got the bed with sheets, a kind of featherbed, while I and the peasant slept in the barn on hay as it was still rather warm. Since my wife's bed was located in the cow shed, her linen was covered with so many fleas that there hardly was any white linen visible; it looked speckled. So my wife went to a small town, Grodzisk Mazowiecki, on foot of course, to buy soap. The town was about eighteen or twenty kilometers away. We took down the sheets and I took a washing board and we soaped the sheets, boiled them, and washed them again and again in hot water until all the dirt was gone and they were white. We then hung them up to dry. Of course we got the peasant's wife's permission to do this.

The farmhouses were spread far apart from each other, some five hundred meters and some two thousand meters. One day I came back to our farmhouse after I went for a walk. My wife told me, "Imagine the meanness of that woman. She took down the sheets of my mattress and pillows and said I should sleep without sheets." I said, "If we are to act like real Aryans, in other words real Poles, we have to take a hard stand." I went to the peasant's wife, whose name I don't remember. She was the boss and set the tone, gave orders and made decisions. Her husband was deaf. I asked, "What is the meaning of this?" "Well, laundry gets ruined from being washed so much"; she could not afford this, and she would not give me any sheets, no matter what. I got upset and I said, "Is this how you treat refugees from Warsaw? It could very well happen that you might become a refugee tomorrow." But nothing helped.

So we went to a neighboring village, crossing fields until we saw another farmhouse. I went inside, while my wife and child stayed outside. I asked if they had shelter. The little house looked very good. I said that we were refugees from Warsaw. Thousands of refugees were passing by and the peasants knew very well what had happened in Warsaw. The peasant's wife agreed. Peasants in general were afraid that the refugees had no money. The peasants felt uncomfortable to eat and have the refugees look on without sharing food with them. Peasants were quite poor and also quite stingy, so that they rarely took anyone in. But the peasant's wife agreed. I said that I had money and would gladly pay her whatever she demanded. The peasant's wife said, "You can have shelter for

Mrs. Ślusarczyk," because I had told her that I looked after the wife of a friend of mine. She said that she would not take money "from you poor refugees." She was a good-hearted woman. There was a room next to the kitchen, which was a bedroom. My wife got a bed there. At first, when the weather was still warm—it was late fall—I slept in the barn. Later on, they made me a sack of straw and put it in my wife's bedroom, so that I would not sleep with her, since I was of course "not her husband." And I did not want to upset the peasants by sleeping with a strange woman, no less the wife of my friend. And that is how we slept; my wife in bed with the child and I in a straw sack on the floor. It was a strange situation.

Piotr Sierociński and his wife, Eleanore, were fine people. They had two girls, one by the name of Władzia and the other one, much younger, was Janina. Everybody was full of lice and cockroaches; it was unnerving. Lice lay their eggs in the hair and our child was full of them, something you could not prevent. My wife went to the pharmacy in the little town of Grodzisk to get advice. She bought kerosene and other kinds of remedies and washed the child's head every day with kerosene. The peasant's family—the wife and the two daughters—deloused themselves once a week and squeezed and crushed the lice. Our beds were full of lice, which we tried to reduce with Lysol. Lice suck as much blood as they can. A neighbor of ours, a man by the name of Jan Tutkiewicz, who was a relative of our peasant, would frequently come and visit us. "Mr. Andrzej," he once told me, "I do not know why Mrs. Zofia tortures the child, washing her hair every day. A healthy child must have lice. Only a sick child has no lice." I just want to point out how backward they were, how uncivilized and ignorant, just like a thousand years ago.

Once a week the women bathed in a wooden tub used to wash laundry. All men were sent to another room. There was no heat in that room and it was cold except for the kitchen where there was an oven for cooking. They also ate quite primitively. For instance, they had one cow, which gave milk; they then took the cream from it to make butter, which they sold along with the milk in town.[1]

---

1 Felicia remembers the cow: "I remember having to watch the cow to make sure she did not go into the wheat field. When she did, I hit her with a stick, which resulted in her going farther into the field. I finally ran into the house crying for help."

They boiled potatoes in water and then added milk to it and ate that without butter. Once a week on Sunday, they slaughtered a rabbit or a chicken and ate some meat and an egg. Every Sunday my child got an egg, as if it were a golden egg. I was able to afford to eat better than that, but I could not, "being a poor refugee," eat better than they did, especially since they did not take any money from me for room and board. Thus, we ate the same as they did. Before baking bread, I ground corn on a millstone. The peasant told me: "Mr. Andrzej, if you want to eat, you have to mill the corn yourself." And so we baked together and ate in a very primitive way. That is what life was like with them.

Now, let me tell you about bathing. I was hardened from home. When I was a child still in elementary school, maybe seven or eight years old, whenever there was fresh snow, my father would wake me up. He always got up at six or six-thirty in the morning, went to the *mikvah* (ritual bath) and then went to pray in the synagogue. At eight he would open the store. So he would wake me when there was fresh snow: "Come, Shloimele. Come outside. You will rub me in." We went out totally naked and I rubbed my father's back and he washed himself in the snow and rubbed me also. Consequently, since childhood I grew up hardened, and even today I hardly ever get a cold.

As mentioned before, whenever the women of the farmhouse bathed, us two men—the head of the household, that is the peasant, and I—went to another room until they were done. Only when a child was bathing could we come in. I washed every day, summer and winter, even when it was minus twenty, thirty, and thirty-five degrees Centigrade. Next to the house was a well where we pulled up water with a chain. I took a bucket, filled it with water, and washed my upper body and legs. I did not wear underpants, but a slip from my wife. I washed up every day after getting up to cleanse the bites from lice and vermin. My buttocks, however, stank, and I was used since childhood to bathe daily, even in cold water. So one Sunday morning at six-thirty—it was winter and still dark—I made a decision. The peasants had already gone to mass. There was a small river not far from our farmhouse. I went and got an axe and chopped through the ice, which was quite thick. The first time I went there to bathe, it took me at least one hour to make a hole with the axe. Since then, every Sunday morning I bathed in the same spot, where the ice was much thinner. When I bathed the first time in the river, I saw from afar people going to the mass. They were about one kilometer away and they could not see my private parts and that I was circumcised. I jogged home in this frost, naked except for the slip, and went inside the kitchen to warm up. One day our neighbor, Mr. Tutkiewicz, who had a few front teeth missing, came in and said: "Mr. Andrzej, I have heard from my grandfather that there are people who bathe under the ice, but neither he nor I have ever seen it. I cannot understand how you of all people can bathe under the ice." I just want to point out such oddities that one had to live through. When the younger daughter, she was about twelve or thirteen years old, saw me come in from the cold and sit next to the stove to warm up, she said loudly: "Mr. Andrzej, watch out, you'll burn your balls." The mother laughed: "Did you hear, old man, what Janina said? She said that Mr. Andrzej will burn his balls."[2]

---

2 Note from Felicia: "When I was in Poland in 1994, I found the farm, met Janina, and was told that to this day people tell the story of my father bathing in the icy river. He has become a local legend. The river, however, is no longer there; it was diverted or dried out. Janina also told how Dad would run from the river and his hair would be frozen and stand up like an icicle. She also mentioned that she would tell Dad he would 'burn his balls.'

24

The Jewish Pigs

Let me tell you the story of the Jewish pigs.

Our peasant was the oldest of the group of peasants. Came winter and peasants had little to do. They could not work the fields, since they were covered with snow and ice. Only the peasants' wives would go early in the mornings to milk the cows, feed the hidden animals, and otherwise prepare food. The animals, such as pigs, were hidden. The peasants rarely went out, and when they did, they would come back early, as it turned dark already around four o'clock. Since they did not go to bed at five o'clock, they would get together at our peasants' place to talk about their problems, about the harvest, the ground, and other issues. The peasants gathered in the kitchen, because the kitchen was the only room that was heated. The other room was not heated. One person would sit on the floor, another on a piece of wood, since there were perhaps only two chairs; and yet there were seven, maybe eight peasants and their families present. One evening, I was casually listening as they were talking about how they fared in the various farmhouses. This peasant was doing fine, another one was not doing well; and they talked about the hidden animals. The German authorities had ordered that every peasant had to hand over to them all pigs and calves. The peasants, however, fattened them and held them illegally.

Then the conversation turned to a certain Mr. S. "Oh, yes," said one of the peasants, "he has Jewish pigs." I was very intrigued. "What do you mean by Jewish pigs?" I asked. That incident occurred before Easter holiday. During Easter, Catholics go to confession to the priest. Tutkiewicz, the relative of my peasant, tried to convince me to go: "Mr. Andrzej, everybody is going to confession. Why are you not going?" "Mr. Tutkiewicz, I will tell you the truth. I studied theology but was not ordained and did not get the priest's cloak. I cannot therefore go to my colleague for confession. But please, don't tell anyone that I was supposed to be a priest." So, I grew in his eyes, and because I told him not to tell anybody, all the inhabitants of the village knew that I was an unordained priest and did not get the priest's cloak. That then was my excuse and Tutkiewicz understood why I could not go to confession to a colleague of mine.

In view of my status as a priest who had not been ordained, I allowed myself to ask the question about the Jewish pigs: "Mr. *Gospodarz*" ("Mr. Host" in Polish, a common way of address in Poland), "what do you mean by Jewish pigs? As far as I know, Jews are not allowed to eat pigs or even to raise them." He replied: "Ach, you are a big-city idiot if you ask such a stupid question," using these exact words. "Why is the question so stupid?" I asked. So, he told me the story of a Jewish family with Aryan papers who came from Grodzisk Mazowiecki to ask this peasant for shelter. The peasant agreed to help. Then, probably out of plain evilness, this peasant notified the Gestapo or the police or the head of the community, that there was a Jewish family in this particular location. And one Sunday there came a whole gang of Gestapos, SS men, and police, maybe also Polish police, though I don't remember anymore. They took the whole Jewish family, three children and their parents, and shot them all to death on the peasant's property. The entire family. Then, they ordered the peasant to bury them in his field. And in their presence, he had to dig a big common grave and bury them. Then they left. After that, from time to time the peasant dug up the grave and gave pieces of body parts to the pigs in order to fatten them up. During the war, fat was scarce. Butter and lard was an expensive commodity, and so he fattened the pigs with Jewish corpses and had the fattest pigs in the area. That is why they were called "Jewish pigs," because they were fattened by Jews.

This gives you some insight of the conditions we were living under. Incidentally, the peasant's wife told me that one night in winter someone knocked on the door. They were Jews who had managed to escape in the bitter winter frost and were pleading for a place to spend the night. They were hungry and frozen. "My old fool," she recounted in his presence, "wanted to take a pitchfork used to pick up dung and go out and kill them. I held him back, put them up in the cow shed, and gave them something warm to drink and to eat, under the condition that they leave at five or at the latest at six o'clock in the morning," since it was dangerous for peasants to hide Jews. Mr. S. was lucky that he was not shot, because he had given shelter to a Jewish family. And that is the way we lived.

In Warsaw we got to know a Christian woman; Alicja was her name. She used to come up to our place on Szucha 11. She was married to a Jew from Kraków and had a child with him. The husband was killed during the Warsaw Uprising and she went back home to her parents or brother, which was close to the farm where we lived. So, from time to time we went through snow and ice to visit her. By the way, when I wanted to exchange dollars, she took care of it, since I did not want to endanger myself. One Sunday we were on our way to visit Alicja, when I saw a man standing in the middle of a field. As we were getting closer to him, we had to go by him, I saw a familiar face: a Jew, an old man. He was at least thirty years older than I. For me, age sixty was old. Today (1981) I am seventy-two years old. The man recognized me: "Oy vey, oy vey, whom do I see here?" And the man started crying. I saw that he was totally drunk, and he continued to cry and speak Yiddish to me: "Oh, to speak a little bit of Yiddish." We were in the middle of a field, and nobody could hear us. He used to be a member of the Bund (Jewish Socialist movement), and he was a Socialist. He even was a very good friend of a certain Adam Ciołkosz, who was the deputy of the Socialist Christian Party in Poland and later became the president of the Polish Government in Exile in London.[1] They were best of friends. He led us to where he lived. He lived with his wife, a daughter, and a son. They were lying on the floor covered with blankets and in *tzures* (Yiddish for "trouble"). That was quite a revelation.[2]

---

1   It could not be verified that Adam Ciołkosz was ever president of the Polish Government in Exile.

2   We are not sure what Dad means by this statement, but probably that it was a revelation to him and Mom that we had much better living conditions.

25

The Liberation of Warsaw

And so we lived with this peasant family until the Russian and Polish army came to Warsaw. The Russian-Polish army (the Polish army was formed by the Communists) crossed the Vistula River and our side of the river was liberated. I still had my last one-hundred-dollar bill, the "last Mohican." We had no clothes; we had nothing. I told my wife to go to Alicja and have her brother change the hundred-dollar bill and exchange fifty dollars for *złotys*, because we had none left, and I was on my way to Warsaw. There were no means of transportation, and so I went on foot, of course. It was winter, and it was cold in Poland, minus twenty-five or thirty degrees Centigrade. I took off for Warsaw to try to retrieve some of our clothes we had hidden in the cellar. On the way I met another Jew, Pelek Perlberger, who was living on Aryan papers. He gave me the news that the Polish *złotys* were made invalid and that the Lublin government, which became the first Polish government, had issued new bills. So I begged him: "Please go and tell my wife not to exchange the money."

I arrived in the house where we had lived in Warsaw, but there was nothing left. The house was turned into rubble and ashes. There was a hole dug through to the cellar, which was probably done by gangs called *Szabrownicy* (Polish for "looters"). During the war and the bombings people hid their entire belongings in their basements in order to protect them. The *Szabrownicy* would dig holes to these underground rooms to steal these goods. We had made a special hiding place. I let myself down through the hole with a lit candle. The ceiling of the cellar was damaged, and there was a danger it would collapse over my head. I discovered that everything was under water. During the bombings, done by the bomb experts, water pipes burst and our whole place was flooded and everything was rotting. My entire effort was for naught. I was able to take something out. I inspected it and it turned out to be underwear and a comforter for our daughter. I carried it out. It was soaked and quite heavy and upon unfolding it, it fell apart as it was all rotted. The only useful item was the comforter. An area in one of its corners was ruined, yet it was still useful for covering the child.

When I came back to the farm, I found out that my wife had already exchanged the fifty dollars and had received twenty-five thousand *złotys* for it, but supposedly they were worthless. It turned out to be true, since the peasants who were aware of the worthless *złotys* refused to sell me anything. The reason my wife had changed the fifty dollars was so we could buy food such as potatoes, but the peasants refused to sell anything for *złotys*. Our peasant said they needed the potatoes for themselves. "Go to that other peasant, he is rich," he said, referring to the one who had fattened the "Jewish pigs" with the Jewish corpses. "He might sell you something." I went to him, but he would not sell any potatoes. "But you know what?" he said. "I can give you two or three potatoes and you can go from peasant to peasant and collect from each two or three potatoes and you'll have something to live on." Well, I saw that it was hopeless; I would not go wandering and beg for potatoes from the peasants. I told my wife that I had heard that on the other side of the Vistula, in Praga, one could get something on the black market for *złotys*. I left her on the farm and walked and crossed over to the other side of the Vistula River to Praga. It was winter and there was an impossible frost. But no one wanted to sell me even one cigarette, not to mention a piece of bread. No one wanted to take the *złotys* from me. I was forced then to go back to the farm, hitchhiking with Russian vehicles. It was February 1945. It was still wartime. The war did not end until May the eighth or ninth of 1945.

On my way back from Praga, I saw people walking and asked where I could stay for the night. Someone told me to go to the police station. I did not know where that was, but someone gave me directions. At the police station they told me that there was no possibility to stay the night as there were thousands of people running about, and they did not have any room. They told me of a Benedictine monastery that was taking in people and that I would be able to stay there for the night. They showed me the way to the monastery. It was night already and everything was covered with ice and snow, but I finally got there. It was a huge building and there were many refugees there. I went in and was met by a Benedictine monk. I told him that I would like to stay overnight. It had been one or two days since I had eaten anything, since I could not buy anything with the *złotys*. So I told the monk that I would like to eat something and asked if he had anything. He answered: "You were here already; leave now, we do not have permanent lodging here." I said: "You are mistaken, Father; I just arrived here today from the other side of the Vistula River and I am here for the first time." "Well," he said, "then go downstairs. There might be some potato soup left." He led me downstairs to the kitchen, where there was a huge pot, but which had only water in it. It looked like dirty water, because it probably was leftover potato soup. He gave me a plate. I asked if he had anything else to eat. He said: "There is some ration bread in the oven still from the Germans. You can try to soak it and see if you can eat it." But I could not even break a piece of bread. It was hard as a brick, impossible to eat. I tried as hard as I could, but it was impossible to break. So I only ate the so-called soup. It was water from potatoes, that's all. Then I went upstairs where there were several people, both men and women. In any event, it was heated, and I could stay the night.

In the morning I realized the hopelessness of my situation. So I thought to myself that I would try to get to my hometown of Tarnów. I had with me two quarter liters of pure home-brewed alcohol made by peasants. Of course it was illegal, but they made it anyway. My peasant gave me the alcohol to use as a payment method. A man who lay next to me in the monastery told me that when you had vodka or schnapps, any Russian driver would give you a ride if you gave it to him. This man clung to me and wanted to go with me under the pretext that I did not know any Russian, not a word of it. I still don't understand much Russian except for a few words that I learned during the short time I spent with Russians. It was about five o'clock in the morning when we left the monastery. There were checkpoints set up by the Russians. All vehicles had to stop at the checkpoints to verify that they had the right to proceed. So, I stood at a checkpoint and waited while the man who had hooked up with me spoke in Russian to the drivers. A large vehicle with several Russians stopped and the man got himself into the truck, which drove off, leaving me behind. I waited for the next vehicle that was heading toward my hometown. It was freezing, maybe thirty-five degrees Centigrade below zero. It had already turned daylight when I saw a Russian officer, probably a major or captain, approach me, and he started speaking Russian to me. I did not understand. He kept talking and pointed toward my ears. Apparently my ears were completely white and the Russian took some snow and rubbed my ears with it. "Otherwise," he said, "you will lose your ears. Your ears will drop off because there is poor blood circulation to them.[1]" He kept on rubbing my ears until they turned red. And so I continued hitchhiking to Tarnów. On the way, the Russian driver took a break. I had given him a quarter liter of alcohol to take me along. They stopped at a bar or some such place where you could get warmed up. There were other hitchhikers among us and everybody got out of the truck. Since I had no money, I remained seated.

---

1 It is unclear as to how Dad understood him. Perhaps Dad guessed what he said.

🗐 Historical Notes

Liberation of Warsaw by the Russians. The following short report appears on the Russian Embassy's website: "On January 17 the Soviet troops liberated the capital Warsaw, though Hitler's orders were that the city should not be surrendered whatever the cost. To mark the liberation of the Polish capital the Presidium of the USSR Supreme Soviet established the medal 'For the Liberation of Warsaw,' which was conferred on more than 682,000 Soviet and Polish soldiers and officers." "The Great Patriotic War (1941–1945)," http://www.russianembassy.org.za/War/1945.html.

Luke Travels: Guide to the World adds further that when the Soviets entered the city, "they found a Warsaw that had almost ceased to exist; 85 percent of the city had been destroyed, including the historic Old Town and the Royal Castle. The surviving Home Army fighters were rounded up by the NKVD (Soviet Secret Police) and either murdered or deported to Siberia." "Warsaw Travel Guide: History of Warsaw Poland," www.luketravels.com/warsaw/history.htm.

 **Visit to Tarnów**

At one of the checkpoints on the way to Tarnów, two armed Russians came up to me and said: "IDs. What are you doing here?" "I am waiting for a hitchhike to go to my hometown," I said. They took me to the Polish military police. At that time there no longer were any conventional policemen. They had been replaced by the military police. When I got there, they asked me: "What do you have with you?" I had the twenty-five thousand *zlotys* from my wife, which I intended to exchange, as well as the last fifty dollars, which was hidden in my jewelry pocket. "Take everything out of your pockets." I took everything out. The man who interrogated me, the MP or captain, said that I should show him my identification card. I showed him the ID and he said, "This is a fake. You are a Jew." "So," I said, "you are an expert in seeking out Jews. Yes, I am a Jew, but today you will not hang me." It was shortly after the departure of the Germans. "We have to confiscate this. You were smuggling money." He accused me of being a smuggler. He noticed by my demeanor that I felt confident in myself. The Gestapo was already gone, and, as a Jew, I believed that I had nothing to fear, though much later on there were many Jews who were sent to Siberia after having survived the Warsaw Uprising and other places. After having accused him of being a specialist in seeking out Jews and as a consequence of my confident demeanor, he said: "All right, go, and take this shit with you." This was a curious occurrence. He dismissed me and I proceeded to Tarnów.

Once in Tarnów, I looked up a PhD in engineering, a friend of mine, to whom I had given all my furniture, clothes, bed linen, and various other things when we had to move to the ghetto. I don't remember anymore, but I think I had also given him silver pieces and watches. I had also given him a silver tray, about ten kilograms in weight. After all, we had a jewelry store that had silver merchandise. He had quite a bit of my fortune and valuables. As I came to his place he was very pleased to see me, and he hugged me. First, he invited me to eat in the pastry shop he owned, and he waited on me. "What can I do for you?" I was wearing a very thin summer coat and a sleeveless shirt with an open collar; all that I had been able to save. That is how I traveled in the frost of thirty to thirty-five degrees Centigrade below zero. Though I was hardened, I was still very cold. So, when he asked me what he could do for me, I said, "You can see how I look; all I own I have on. I need money. I have merchandise with you." Among the things he had from me were platinum as well as gold items, which he said he had all melted down. He said, "The war is not yet over. The Germans are gone, but the Russians are here." He asked me what I needed urgently. "I urgently need money, at least two hundred dollars," I said. "OK, wait," he said, and he brought me the money. Two hundred dollars was an absolute fortune for me. All I had left was one fifty-dollar bill. I got the two hundred dollars and, by the way, that was all I ever got back from him. In the meantime he was arrested as a *Volksdeutsche*. With the Russians in control, the Poles "took care" of him.

27

Struggle in Lublin

I hitchhiked back home via Lublin where the new Polish government, which had been formed after the war, was in power. In Lublin I found out that they were paying five hundred *złotys* for the dollar, while by us in Warsaw we did not yet have the new Lubliner money. So, I thought to myself that I would change my two hundred and fifty dollars on the black market, and when I came to Warsaw, I could buy back dollars for almost half the price.[1]

Here is something very interesting. As I mentioned earlier I hitchhiked to Lublin on my way from Tarnów.[2] There the snow was forty to fifty centimeters high. There were still mandatory blackouts. We arrived at night, and they let me out of the vehicle. It was completely dark, and I did not know where to go. The shoes I had on were made out of rubber from car tires. Instead of leather, the soles were made from rubber. My wife had bought me the shoes in the marketplace in Grodzisk Mazowiecki. They were two or three sizes too big on me. They were used shoes, but my old ones were already useless. Anyway, whenever I took a step, the shoe would get stuck in the snow. I did not know what to do. I saw a sliver of light coming out of a shack. It was some kind of store where they were selling various things. I asked them to give me some cloth because my shoes kept getting stuck in the snow. He gave me some rope, but it was woven out of paper. I tied my feet to the shoes, but on the way, the rope became

---

1 Since the old *złotys* were supposedly worthless in Warsaw Dad presumably changed the dollar to the new Lubliner *złotys*. Dad says that during the war the Polish currency was called "Lenarski," named after the German finance minister in charge of that area. The Lenarski was also worthless now.
2 Dad explains later that he made two other trips from Warsaw to Lublin as well.

soaked, and I again had *tzures* (trouble) with my shoes. At last, I heard voices; two people were talking in Polish. As I listened, one voice sounded familiar. It was that of a jewelry supplier of mine from Warsaw, from whom we used to buy merchandise. I recognized him right away, though I forget his name now. So I called out his name and he said, "Who is there?" I gave my name. Oh, he was so happy. He used to come to our store every month to sell us merchandise. He led me to the Jewish community center. There were people who had come out of the forest and from Russia as well as others who had somehow survived. They had set up boards to sleep on, but everything was infested with lice. First, I went to the administration. The men there had a sense of humor; everybody was laughing. I too laughed at my own predicament. When they asked me for my name I said Schlomek Białecki, Białecki being my Polish name. They offered to have me sleep over, but I told them I could not because of the lice. I asked them for permission to place three stools together to sleep on, but they would not let me because it was an office. It was impossible.

Everyone was filthy. The partisans who had come out of the forest relieved themselves wherever they happened to be. The stench was terrible. Somehow, people had managed to live through this. I went to a Russian store and bought rice, vodka, and other food items.[3] While I was there I found out that the Jewish Community of Lublin had received packages of "love donations" (care packages), such as of suits, underwear, pajamas, and so forth. These "love donations" came from all over the world, but mainly from England and America. I was told to come early the next morning and that I would receive necessities, as my wife and child had absolutely nothing. The crates supposedly had arrived but had not yet been opened. When I came the next morning to the office there were perhaps twenty or thirty people waiting. The chairman of the community was not to be seen. It was eight o'clock, and then nine o'clock, and everybody waited. Finally at nine-thirty or ten o'clock, he arrived. Everyone received fifty or one hundred *złotys*, I do not remember the exact amount. As to clothing, however, we were told to come in one or two days. It was then that I made a scene. I said, "The crates have arrived for us, and I demand that I get to them

---

3 Dad recalls below that this might have happened later.

right away." I made a scene, and he took it to heart and tried to calm me down. He gave me I believe a pair of trousers and a pair of shoes, which I put on right away. My old shoes were only good enough to be thrown away. There was a dress and underwear for my wife and a dress for my child. My child was five years old; it was 1945.

I also had a leather briefcase, which I brought with me to Lublin. It was made out of rather thick leather. That was still before I had changed the dollars. I needed money in order to buy something to eat, since my wife and child were hungry. Someone advised me: "Oh, you have a leather briefcase. Go to the marketplace. It is worth a lot; there you can get money for it. They can make soles for shoes from the leather." I asked him: "How does this work over there?" "Hold on to your briefcase, and you'll see people will come to you and make you an offer." In fact, I went and stood there with the briefcase. A Pole came up to me and wanted to know how much I wanted for it. I did not know how much to ask for it—perhaps a thousand *złotys*? We agreed upon a price. I don't remember anymore how much it was, but it was the first of the new money I got hold of, money that was worth something. For this money I bought a backpack made of cloth in that marketplace. I bought food and put it and the care packages into the backpack.

These are stories that happened in 1945; that was thirty-six years ago. I had heard that a convoy of Polish government employees was going to Warsaw, because the Polish government was being transferred from Lublin to Warsaw. There were no trains yet. The people loaded up everything possible, such as office desks and chairs, for setting up this government. Among the people involved were also Jews. They promised me that I could join the convoy of trucks, which would take me to Warsaw. It really happened; after a wait of one or two days, they took me along to Warsaw. The convoy drove with their lights dimmed. The trucks were fully loaded and I sat on top of a dresser, all the way up high, since there was no other choice due to lack of space. There were five or six trucks in the convoy. We drove at night. Suddenly, we heard planes, and the truck lights were turned off. We saw bombs fall on villages. The Germans were still staging an attack. We were all ordered to get down, to get out of the trucks. I could not get down; it was impossible. Those who could ran into the field and hid. Later, we drove with our lights off. There were perhaps twenty or thirty huge fires raging where bombs had fallen, such as on stables and peasant huts. Everything was engulfed in huge fires. There was nothing to save; everything was incinerated.

Actually, I was in Lublin twice. The first time I was there I returned with the truck convoy. The second time I was there I received the care packages and took the train back to Warsaw. Anyway, the fact remains that I found out that there was a train going to Warsaw, the first train to go there. I got into the train with the backpack and a bag with bread. The train was unbelievably packed because there were no other means of transportation, no way to drive, no buses, and no other possibilities. We were all pressed against each other. The trip from Lublin normally took about four hours; yet we rode three days and nights. The train stood still more often than it moved, since they were repairing the railroad tracks. While still in Lublin, there was a brownout, and the train there was in total darkness. I could not carry the backpack on my back because there was no room. Therefore, I placed it and the bread bag between my feet. Suddenly someone yelled in Russian to make room for Russian soldiers who had to get through. So I made room by moving to the side. As soon as they went through I looked for my backpack and it was gone. It had disappeared. The Russians had taken it. It had been totally dark but they had lanterns so that they could see. Of the care packages, only the shoes that I wore were left, while all the clothing and the backpack was gone. The only thing I brought home was rice, which I had bought at the Russian store, and, of course, the money.

I want to mention to you the Szpilman family who had helped my wife and child when they arrived to Milanówek on Aryan papers. The family was in the candle manufacturing business and had been very wealthy. By the way, I had saved the father, Abraham Szpilman, and a daughter -in-law during the second deportation. They had two sons: Monek Spzilman, whose Aryan name was Karol Szpalski, and Henryk. Before the war, Monek was an artist; he performed in the theater and wrote poems for newspapers. He was also a scientist. Monek was truly from the "golden youth." His brother Henryk was president of the chamber of commerce in Tarnów. They were truly the elite. When I came to the Jewish Community in Lublin, I met an acquaintance from Tarnów. I forget now who that was. He told me that the Szpilman family lived in a small village outside Warsaw. On my way back to Warsaw I met my friend Perlberger, who told me of a tragedy that befell the Szpilmans. One of their sons was killed by a Russian bomb dropped from an airplane just before the end of the war. The Russian and Polish army had not moved until January 15, 1945. They then bombed smaller towns and villages, since Warsaw already was in soot and ashes. The younger son, Monek, had some merchandise, namely sewing needles that he had smuggled from Częstochowa. Henryk was to deliver them to a clothing store in Grodzisk Mazowiecki. When he got off the train there was an air raid. He ran into a store for cover, but a bomb killed him.

With the money I brought from Tarnów I started to trade in currencies. I bought dollars for one-half of the amount I had exchanged in Lublin. I took, let's say two hundred or three hundred *złotys*, bought dollars, and then hitch-hiked to Lublin and got five hundred *złotys* for them. Over time the price difference in Lublin became smaller as the currency evened itself out. That is how I earned my first dollars. I made four hundred or five hundred dollars out of two hundred and fifty. It was my first business venture.

 **Historical Notes**

According to a post on the alinaselyukh.wordpress.com wesite, the term **Golden Youth** "is a cliché overused in Russian socio-political, youth-related or pop-culture-observational analyses. Leaking into common language, the notion of "golden youth" has long shifted from a set phrase or a group definition to an easily recognized social phenomenon with two definitions: 1. Outstandingly bright, goal- and career-oriented representatives of a promising young generation; 2. Children of successful, rich and prominent parents, who usually subsist on their wealth and connections." http://alinaselyukh.wordpress.com/2008/09/17/the-golden-youth. Updated September 17, 2008.

Lublin. In her article "The Virtual Jewish History Tour, Lublin," Rebecca Weiner, a leading expert on the Jewish communities of Poland, writes that Lublin "was the first city liberated in Poland by the Russian army on July 24, 1944, and served as a temporary Polish capital until the liberation of Warsaw. After the war, 5,000 Jews settled in Lublin, but many left the city between 1946 and 1950 because of anti-Semitism. Today, there are only about 60 Jews, all of them over the age of 55, in the city." Jewish Virtual Library, http://www.jewishvirtuallibrary.org/jsource/vjw/Lublin.html.

Jewish Lublin, 1945. In her memoir, *Dry Tears: The Story of a Lost Childhood*, Dr. Nechama Tec describes her family's survival in Poland under Aryan papers. She then depicts their return to her hometown, Lublin together with her and her survivor parents. They go to her family's chemical factory and Dr. Tec describes her feelings of fear and dscomfort as her father knocks on their former janitor's door of. "Their expression of surprise was followed by an uneasy smile: 'You are alive … ? Welcome, welcome, make yourself comfortable here. Yes, there were many Jews still alive in Lublin. They came back from all over. The Jews were very rich. And the Russians were giving them all kinds of privileges. They had it good. There is a special center where all the Jews go to find relatives." Nachama sees many of her family's belongings in the janitor's apartment having "become a part of someone else's lives. ... Their settled presence made me feel like an intruder." Her family then goes to the Jewish Center located in a "run-down building on one of those dark and narrow streets. ... The center consisted of three small rooms. The walls were covered with differently shaped papers that had messages, names, and addresses scribbled all over them. Poorly lit and poorly ventilated, the place was filled with people, talking and gesticulating in Polish, Yiddish, Hungarian, and languages I could not recognize" *Dry Tears: The Story of a Lost Childhood*, Oxford: Oxford University Press, 1984, pages 218–222.

Russian occupation. As the website Polish Resistance explains, "The end of the German occupation turned out to be the start of a new occupation—this time by the Soviets. Despite the Delegature [Polish government in exile] and AK's [Polish Home Army] efforts ... [t]he functioning of the Polish Underground State was halted at the most critical moment. ... At Yalta the Allies conceded dominance of Central Europe to Soviet Union, which facilitated the destruction of the Polish Underground State. On 21 June 1945 Stalin created in Moscow a Polish puppet regime called the Provisional Government of National Unity. G. Ostasz, "The Polish Government-in-Exile's Home Delegature," http://www. polishresistance-ak.org/17%20Article.htm.

28

Going to Łódź

I had heard that the city of Łódź, the Germans called it Litzmanstadt, had not been bombed during the war and therefore had not been damaged. So, I decided to go there. Interestingly, I found out that the chief editor of the military paper was a former friend of mine from *Hashomer Hatzair*, which is a Jewish scout organization. His name had been Heschek Stramer; now it was Major Werner. He had come back from Russia and became a Communist. He was now in Łódź. When I heard that my friend was such an important personality and that Łódź had not been bombed, I said to my wife, "We are going to Łódź." The trains were running already, but we did not go with a passenger train but rather with a coal-carrying train with open wagons. We arrived in Łódź, I and my wife with the child, our daughter, who today is a *Rebbetzen* (rabbi's wife). Somebody had given me Heschek's address in Łódź. In any case some Jew took us in and gave us a couch to stay overnight. The three of us, my wife with the child next to her and I on the other side, slept on the couch.

I wanted to know where to find Heschek. I found out from somebody that the main publisher's office of *Polska Zbrojna* (Polish Armed Forces), a military newspaper, was located on the main street. First, however, I found out where he lived, and I went to his apartment. It was evening and it was raining heavily. I only had a light coat on, which was totally soaked through. It was March. I got to the street where he lived, called Ulica Literacka, or Literary Street. I found the correct house number and went upstairs to the second floor and rang the bell. His sister, a young girl of maybe twenty, opened the door. I said, "Wella," which was her name, "do you know who I am?" "Yes," she said, "you had a jewelry store on Krakowska Street. Your name is Lederberger. What would you like?" I said, "I would like to speak with your brother Heschek." She left me standing in the entrance hall, not inviting me in, and went back into the apartment. Her husband or fiancé came out and told me that Heschek had a bigwig with him and could not see me now. I should go to the publishing office the next day. He had a large apartment because of his high position. An editor-in-chief of a military paper was a big shot. I came home soaked, not even having been invited for a cup of tea. I caught a cold and had high fever, which happened rarely, as I was very hardened. I lay for several days on the couch until the fever was gone.

I went to visit Heschek in the publishing office. The entrance downstairs was guarded by two guards with submachine guns. Inside the building was a doorman: "Where do you want to go?" I had to fill out my name and he noted the exact time—eleven o'clock and twelve minutes—and whom I wanted to see. Then he indicated that I could go upstairs to the second floor. In front of his door on the second floor was another armed guard. I knocked and entered the room. Heschek was sitting behind a huge desk. Also present was another man from Tarnów, an attorney by the name of Emil Mertz, who was the brother of Juliusz Mertz, who had disappeared in Warsaw together with Jadźka Bramowicz.

"Good morning," I said, "do you recognize me, Heschek?" He said, "You are Schlomek Lederberger," using the formal third person to address me: "you" (*Sie*), while I addressed him with the informal "you" (*Du*). His first question was, "How come they gassed all the Jews, and you are alive?" He asked in a suspicious manner. I said, "Heschek, do I have to apologize that I survived?" He said, "No, but it is strange; only collaborators survived." When he saw my reaction, which was of righteousness and self-confidence, he became milder. Initially he interrogated me like the NKWD (Russian secret service), and I responded in a straightforward manner. I was just a poor devil and he such a big shot; our situations could not be compared. It was humorous that I addressed him in the informal *Du*, while he addressed me in the formal *Sie*.

Then the lawyer asked me if I knew whether his wife and daughter had survived. His daughter, who also had belonged to *Hashomer Hatzair*, always used to come by the store with a nurse. The daughter used to call me *Pan Pierścionek* (Polish for "Mr. Ring man"). I told him, "They were killed without any doubt." Then Heschek asked me, "What can I do for you?" I said, "Heschek, as I told you, I saved myself, my wife, and my child, and I would like to have a roof over my head. I heard that you are a big shot and that you can help me." He answered me that he could not help me: "I am too big of a big shot to demand special favors from my subordinates for a Tarnower. However," he said, "there is a young man from Tarnów who helps people from Tarnów. He can help you." Heschek gave me the address of an engineer. He was the son of the man I met in the field in a drunken state some time earlier. The son was a big shot and probably a Communist. His father was a Socialist. The son was the manager of all industries in Łódź and surrounding. "He has the highest position, and he will help you," Heschek said. I thanked him and went to see the engineer. His assumed name was engineer Malinowski. His real name was Leibel. The Russians exerted pressure from above to drop one's Jewish name. When someone came with an existing Jewish name he was required to adopt a Polish name. I went upstairs to see him. Again the same story: guards with submachine guns and filling out papers with who I was, whom I wanted to see, and so forth. I said "Engineer Malinowki" and I went in. He recognized me though he was not in my age group; he was much younger than I. I had been a friend of his father's, but the two of us knew each other only by sight. He greeted me and began to talk very politely: What could he do for me? I said, "A roof over my head." He said, "Yes, I can help you. I will appoint you the director of five textile factories. You will automatically get a suite in the best hotel in Łódź"—I think it was the Savoy—"until an apartment can be found for you. You will also get food, other provisions, and anything you need for your family." I told him, "Mr. Engineer Malinowski, I have never in my life seen a weaving loom and you want me to become director of five textile factories? I have no understanding of it."

"That does not matter; you don't need to know anything. You will get a secretary, and you will be fine." I said, "I thank you very much, but I cannot accept it, also for other reasons. First of all, I have no understanding of textile manufacturing. The janitor of the factory would know more than the director himself. I don't feel comfortable doing this. Second, you know the circumstances; whenever someone gets a high position, such as the directorship, he automatically gets enrolled as member in the Communist Party. That I won't like, because I never belonged to any party. Besides, at the first opportunity I get I want to leave the country. I want to go to America where I have relatives." He answered that it was almost impossible to get me an apartment otherwise. He said that he had a good friend, probably also a Jew, who was responsible for assigning apartments and hotel rooms, but that without a title and official position, Malinowski could not demand he give me an apartment, since that would be considered bribery. I thanked him and did not accept his offer.

I managed to sublease a room in an attic. I looked around the city and saw a (empty) watch store in a big building located on the main street at Piotrkowska, number 1. A Russian guard stood in front of the building. Then, by chance, I met a former client of mine from my hometown. She was a Christian woman and a very nice person. She recognized me on the street and was happy to see me and we talked. She was waiting for her husband, who was a high-ranking officer in the Polish army, but he also spoke Russian fluently. He was probably a Communist, because he wore a Russian uniform of a lieutenant.[1] She introduced me to him. It must have been her second husband, since her first husband had been an engineer in Tarnów where he had worked in a chemical plant. I asked him if he could help me out. I knew no Russian, and there was a line of perhaps a thousand people or more waiting for assignments of apartments and business spaces. Those assignments had not been made yet. The assignments were under the direction of the war commander, who was a Russian. Her husband asked me how he could be of help. I told him of my situation, namely that I was a watchmaker. I did not want to reveal that I really was a goldsmith and jeweler, though my father had been a watchmaker and I understood the craft. I thought to myself that things might not work well for me as a goldsmith under the Communist regime, because jewelry was regarded as a luxury. So, I claimed that I was a watchmaker and the Russians considered watches a dream item. The building in which the watchmaker store was located was guarded by a Russian soldier. The Russians had confiscated the entire building, though the store was empty except for some furniture.

---

1 Inconsistency: Said to be in the Polish army, but in a Russian uniform.

I told the lieutenant that I had seen a storefront and that I needed to start making some money, and I asked if he could help me. He said, "Listen, buy a liter of vodka, and I will introduce you to the assistant of the war commander, who is a friend of mine," and he would get me in. He then led me around the line since he was wearing a uniform. He took me to the assistant of the war commander and told him in Russian what this was all about—that I had seen a watchmaker store in that building, which was occupied by the Russians—and asked him if he could help assign the store to me. The assistant told me to come the next day and to bring him a bottle of vodka. I got a liter of vodka, came in the next day, and slipped it to the assistant, who put it in his desk drawer. He then took out an assignment form for those premises. The note said that I may enter and take over the store. I went to the store and entered it. There was furniture, but no tools; no screwdrivers, no tweezers, absolutely nothing. What good did it do me? The war was still going on, and I could not buy the needed tools; that was impossible; and I could not repair watches with my fingers.

📑 Historical Notes

Łódź. Miriam Weiner reports on the Jewish community in Łódź in her book *Jewish Roots in Poland: Pages from the Past and Archival Inventories* (Secaucus, NJ: Miriam Weiner Routes to Roots Foundation and the YIVO Institute for Jewish Research, 1997). "In the immediate postwar period, some 38,000 Jews settled in Łódź, making it Poland's most important Jewish community. However, confronted by economic hardship, political violence, repression, and anti-Jewish hostility, most of this community emigrated."

29

The Road to Danzig

I saw a headline in a newspaper that the city of Danzig had been liberated without a shot fired. So I said to my wife, "I will go to Danzig. The Germans capitulated without one bullet being fired; that is what the headlines said." I figured that there I might get hold of tools, buying them or finding them. I went back to Major Werner and told him that I would like to go to Danzig. Meanwhile, Szpilman, whose brother was killed in Grodzisk Mazowiecki by a bomb, was in Łódź. He was a friend of Major Werner, the chief editor of the military newspaper. Major Werner learned from Szpilman that I had "behaved myself" during the war. Szpilman told him that I had saved several hundred people, including his parents; that I had handled myself in a first-class manner, having saved Jews, wherever I could; that I had "behaved myself" very well indeed; that I had not been a collaborator. I asked Major Werner if he could provide me with the means to get to Danzig. The war was still ongoing and the German military was still in the Hel Peninsula in the Baltic Sea. The Germans had retreated to that peninsula and had dug in. He told me that as soon as the office of the editor sent a team to Danzig, and if I got a pass from the war command post, he could take me along. I obtained a pass through the assistant of the war commander, which cost me one liter of vodka. One day a representative from the office of the editor notified me they were sending a team in two large vehicles to Danzig. There were perhaps fifteen or twenty people in our group, editors and journalists; all were in Polish military uniforms. They were supposed to put me in a uniform as well, but before departing the following day, no uniform was available. So they instructed me to go to the corner of the vehicle, as there were checkpoints every fifteen, twenty, or thirty kilometers at which we were stopped and the driver had to show a permit to go to Danzig.

I arrived in Danzig with the team. Danzig was emptied of inhabitants. There were few civilians to be seen. Danzig lay smoldering in a heap of ruins. We arrived and slept in an empty house. The team left, since they had to go to the front where the fighting took place and report on the situation. Houses that had not been bombed out stood empty, some with crystal and silver items in plain sight. The team loaded up on whatever they saw: typewriters, porcelain, and other valuables. They hoarded all they could. I would have also taken some things, but I had no apartment and no car to store the goods. I started to look around and to assess the situation. The team took off and left. Heaps of ruins were everywhere. Eventually I met a civilian and asked him to show me where a watchmaker store had been located. He said that he would tell me if I got him some bread, which I did. He showed me where there had been a watchmaker store, but it was a pile of ruble. There were destroyed houses on both sides of the streets.

I met an elderly civilian. He carried a little handbag as physicians do, and he was crying. Why was he crying? He was a dentist. He then recounted what had happened. Hitler had given the order that whenever the Germans retreated from a city they were to leave it in soot and ashes. The mayor of Danzig decided, however, that in order to save the city which was the richest in Germany and Poland, they would not offer any resistance; they would not defend themselves. Danzig was a corridor, an open window to the whole world. Ships came from all over the world to bring as well as to load up on merchandise. Its citizens were stinking rich; many were multimillionaires. The dentist told me that the Russians came in without firing a shot. Everywhere white flags were flying; there was no resistance as they feared that otherwise they would be bombed. Before the Russians came in, the citizens of Danzig took all their valuables, such as crystal, silver, rugs, and sewing machines, hoarded all these goods, and bought more, since they were afraid that their money would be devalued. Thus, in one house for instance, one would find twenty typewriters, ten sewing machines, or five new refrigerators. They placed the most valuable items in the basements; so, in case of bombings their goods would be saved.

However, when the Russians, along with the Polish army, arrived in Danzig and surrounding towns, including the town of Sopot, they expelled all the civilian population of Danzig beyond a twenty to thirty kilometer fenced-in perimeter and left them without shelter. Then, they came in with trucks and took all the goods and possessions, including pianos, from the homes and basements of the entire population of Danzig and loaded them up onto trucks. There were hundreds of trucks, all driving in the direction of the harbor, where the goods were loaded onto Russian ships that sailed off to Russia. Later on, after they had looted everything, the Russians sent in platoons of explosives experts, rigged entire blocks, and blew them up. The dentist told me that he had been taken out of the barbed-wired compound, along with his instruments, because a high-ranking officer had a toothache. He had helped the officer by pulling out his aching tooth or performed some other procedure, and in return, he was let free to go back to Danzig. He said that when he left Danzig, his house had been intact. Now, he could not find the street nor the house, because there were no houses left. His house had been in the center of the city. He was homeless and that was why he was crying. He had thought himself lucky to be released, but now he had no place to go; his whole house was gone. After having taken over Danzig, the Russians mined it and reduced it to a pile of rubble. Then they officially handed it over to Poland, as had been agreed upon in Yalta with Stalin, Churchill, and Roosevelt: that the corridor would be handed over to Poland. Only after having destroyed Danzig did they ceremoniously turn over the city to Poland.

Now I went in search of tools. The man whom I had met earlier in Danzig took me to a major business center at the outskirts of town. I gave him some bread in return. But the place was a heap of rubble. The man went away, and I was left among the rubble. There were still some walls standing. The man had told me that this place had been the center of a large watchmaking company. I then saw a safe among the rubble, which was untouched. I saw other safes that had been ripped open like cans of sardines. Only this one safe was intact. It was huge. I thought I got lucky. But how to break open the safe? You had to be a burglar to know how to open such a safe. How do I go about it? I kept thinking about what to do. I had no contacts. I wracked my brain. Then I decided that it was best to take the straight path. I would go to the Russian war commander, tell him that I used to have a watchmaker and jewelry store; that I was search-ing for tools; that I had discovered a safe. I would tell him that we would split everything fifty-fifty. That was the only way I could think of getting it opened. I found out where the commander was and asked to see him. There were guards everywhere. "I have an important message for him," I said.

Finally, I got to see his assistant, a major. He asked me to tell him what it was all about. I said, "No, I want to talk to the commander personally." He went to the next room and got the colonel, a Russian colonel. I explained to him that I had a business in the past, that I was a master watchmaker and had come in search of tools and had found a safe. He wanted me to tell him where it was. I said, "I will tell you, but you have to give me your word of honor as an officer that everything will be split fifty-fifty. Otherwise I won't tell you where it is." At last he shook hands with me and said, "You have my word of honor as an officer that everything will be split fifty-fifty. How do I get to open it?" I told him that I had seen a welding machine in the Polish barracks. I saw them work with a welding tool. "Colonel, you are the chief of Danzig," I told him. "I saw a welding machine in the Polish army barrack." He wanted me to tell him where the safe was. He had after all given me his word of honor, so I told him where the safe was. We then went right away together to see it. He told me to come back next morning at 7:30 and that we would go to the safe together. The next day I got to the command post at 7:30 a.m. I told them I had an appointment with the commander. They told me to sit down. They let me sit. Meanwhile, I saw how they were interrogating private citizens to get information. They beat them, old people in their nineties. They were forced to put on a hood, part of an old knight's armor. They made fun of the people and beat them. As I was watching this, I looked at my watch. I still had my watch. It was already 9:30 a.m. Somehow, my gut feeling told me I should run over to the safe. It was getting ridiculous; neither the assistant nor the commander had shown up and I was sitting like an idiot and waiting. They kept telling me to sit. I told them I was hungry. They wanted to give me vodka to drink. Finally, I told them that I had to go home. I lived on the outskirts, subletting from a man from Danzig. I ran straight to the safe. When I arrived, I saw a huge truck parked on the rubble. The safe was ripped wide open, welded wide open. As I climbed up the bricks I saw the commander, who looked at me holding a silver pen in his hands. It was a lady's pen. While twirling the pen he said, "There was nothing in the safe." The back of the truck was closed so that I could not see inside. The safe was already emptied and he said, "There was nothing." Then he handed me the silver pen and said, "That's for you." That is what I got for his word of honor. He had cleaned out everything.

It was then that I realized what a stupid thing I had done. They could have shot me like a cat and let me rot. You could see dead people hanging from trees. When we arrived in Danzig with the team, we saw young boys hanging from trees with a sign attached to them: "I was a coward." There were dead horses lying in the middle of the street, as well as corpses.

Now, something interesting happened. At first I stayed in Langfuhr, today known as Wrzeszcz, which is on the outskirts of Danzig. It was destroyed just as Danzig proper was; yet, here and there stood houses with gardens that were intact and that were of course used by the Russian war commanders. All houses on major streets, such as the Belgelei here in Antwerp, were completely destroyed.[1] Even churches lay in ruins.

I hitchhiked from Langfuhr to Sopot.[2] In Sopot I stayed with a family, an elderly couple. I saw an apartment and went in. The man and his wife, Mr. and Mrs. Krüger, were shaking from fear, because there were many robbers, both Poles and Russians, who entered into apartments and robbed everything. They would tell the people to turn around, then beat them and rob them. There was no police or military to impose order; there was total *tohu wawohu* (Hebrew for "chaos"). I asked the Krügers if I could stay with them and said that I would protect them. I wrote a note stating: "Here resides the Pole Andrzej Białecki, the official employee of the Łódź chamber of commerce. Any entry is strictly prohibited." I pasted the notice on the front door. That is what I wrote, and the family was grateful to me.

I went back and forth between Langfuhr and Sopot on foot. There were checkpoints. The first time I went from Langfuhr to Sopot, or the other way

---

1 Belgelei is a wide and fancy boulevard in Antwerp. Our parents lived off Belgelei, at Charlottellei 51.
2 Town located on the Baltic Sea, known as a resort town.

around, they stopped me and a guard with a submachine gun asked me, "Where are you going?" I said that I was going to work. He asked if I had a pass. I took out the pass from the commander in Łódź, which gave me permission to go to Danzig. The guard took the pass, threw it into the trash can, and searched me. I had bread and smoked meat and a quarter liter of vodka with me. He took everything away and locked me in a room. The room was filled with people. Among them was a team of the Polish government. They probably were traveling by car, were stopped, told to get out, and locked up in that room. I was the last to be locked up, because there was no more room. There was also a man in a white coat from the Red Cross. He was a doctor who, with his assistant, was on his way in a horse-drawn carriage to see very sick and injured people. So, we talked. I don't remember how many people there were, perhaps forty or perhaps fifty or sixty. It was barely possible to turn around. The guard had bolted the door shut. We decided that the first person to be let out would report to the war commander as to what was going on, that the guard was arresting everybody. By the way, the guard also took away my watch, the pen I had, as well as tobacco from my backpack. He took away everything, and then threw my pass into the wastebasket. After one or two hours, the guard opened the door. He was totally drunk; he probably had finished off my vodka. He addressed me first: "Where are you going?" "I was on my way to work. I gave you my pass," I said. "Get out of here! Get lost! Beat it!" he said. The next person he talked to was the physician from the Red Cross and his assistant. He showed the guard documents that he was from the Red Cross and that he was a doctor on his way to see a sick person. He told him to get lost as well. As we came out the doctor said to me, "We are going to the commander. He'll know what to do. There are people in there locked up who were appointed by the Polish government (the *Wojewoda*). to set in place a team to supervise shipping activity." He had a horse-drawn wagon. I sat down in it and we rode to the commander. I was the representative since the doctor spoke only German, being from Danzig. I told the guards that we were representatives of the region. They led us to the war commander. We told him why we had come, the conditions at the checkpoint, how the guard there was locking up people sent by the Polish government, and that he was taking everything away from everybody, including my watch. The commander then ordered his assistant, a major, to go out there. The major did not want to get into the carriage. Instead, he mounted a bicycle and we all went to the checkpoint. The major said to the guard: "Misza, what are you doing?" I think that is what he said as I don't speak Russian. He ordered him to unlock the door and let everyone out. Then I said, "I want my watch and pen." He said he had not taken anything. I told him that he had put my things in the desk drawer, and I opened the drawer. The guard gave me a dirty look, because he could have shot me. Anyhow, I got my belongings back except for the vodka and tobacco, which had disappeared. Well, that is not important. Anyway, I kept going back and forth between Langfuhr and Sopot.

One day, as I was walking from Langfuhr to Sopot, I saw a group of women dressed in concentration camp clothing across the street, their heads shaved. It was about the end of March 1945, and there was still snow and ice on the ground. They were dragging their bodies along, and everybody was turning around to look at them. There were perhaps five or six women. One of the women was being held up by others because she could not walk. They were all skeletons, severely starved. I stopped for a moment and one of the women ran over to me and said, "Schlomek." My name is Salomon, but I was called Schlomek. I did not recognize her. She was a girl who along with her mother had been expelled from Germany in 1938. At that time Hitler had pushed out all Polish citizens living in Germany to Poland. Her name was Jenia. I don't know her last name. "Jenia," I said, "what is going on?" She told me that they had been in Stutthof, in the concentration camp, and that they had been freed. Prisoners who were found alive in the French, American, and English zones were cared for, taken to hospitals, given food and a roof over their head. Those who survived on the Russian and Polish side were just freed and received no support. The Poles had no say whatsoever, and all officers who wore Polish uniforms were in fact Russians and they did nothing for the prisoners. Some of them could speak Polish quite well, and some did so poorly and with a Russian accent. Then another girl came over. She did not know me and I did not know her. I had already moved in with the Krüger family in Sopot. So I said, "Come with me." I took them all up to the apartment, where I had put up the sign. Of course, I notified Mrs. Krüger and asked her to make some tea and something to eat. There was no coffee available. The women went first to the bathroom to wash up. One of the women lay down right away, because she could not stand up. They were all emaciated like skeletons. Here at last they were able to get some sleep, two or three to a bed, as there were not enough beds. The next day I told Mrs. Krüger to take down the drapes, so that they could sew themselves some dresses, as there was no cloth to be had. There was total *tohu wawohu*. Everything was destroyed. They sewed themselves some clothes and underwear. Thus, I provided them with first aid, mainly a roof over their heads. I then tried to get one of the women, who was very ill, admitted to the hospital. I don't remember how I did it, but they took her in. I just want to emphasize the difference between the Russians and the Western powers. The Russians did not help the freed prisoners whatsoever; they did not provide any food or shelter. It was terrible. Later on I saw "love packages" arrive from all over the world, but not into the Russian zone, only the English zones.

🗐 Historical Notes

Stutthof. According to the website Jewishgen.org, Stutthof, located thirty-four kilometers from Danzig, was the first concentration camp created by the Nazis outside of Germany (September 2, 1939) and the last camp liberated by the Allies (May 10, 1945). The first prisoners to arrive at the camp included 250 Polish citizens and POWs. Two weeks later, on September 15, 1939, some 6,000 prisoners were in the camp, most of whom were later executed. Vincent Châtel and Chuck Ferree, "The Forgotten Camps," www.jewishgen.org/ForgottenCamps.

Danzig. The Russians took over Danzig in March 1945. At that time roughly 90 percent of the city was reduced to ruins. By the end of the war, an estimated 90 percent of the population were either dead or had fled to other parts of the country and the world. Felicia visited Danzig in 1994. They have rebuilt the old city as it was before WWII.

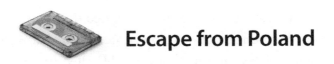

30

Escape from Poland

In Sopot I searched around and found an optical store that had machines to polish lenses. Using some cunning, I received the first business allocation in Sopot. Getting the business allocation was of primary importance. I declared that I was a master optician, though I had never had anything to do with being an optician. I saw that store, however, and thought to myself, "I won't make it as a jeweler. Only as an optician and watchmaker," which went hand in hand, "will I succeed." So, I declared that I was a master optician. The mayor of Sopot happened to wear glasses, and as soon as he heard about my plans, he asked me to see him right away. He told me that he would do his best to protect the store, as everything was in rubble. The windows of the store were shattered, and everything had been robbed. I received the official allocation after the end of the war—the first in Sopot—around the middle of May, and things started moving up for me. My wife was still in Łódź with our child. In the meantime I restored the shop, including the windows. Since there was no mail, I let my wife know that I was in Sopot by giving someone in the military my address. Later on, she arrived in Sopot with our child.

My store started to flourish. Primarily, I supplied eyeglasses to the national health insurance. Then, people from Danzig started to come, as well as people who had been expelled from Danzig and were living in camps. People could not start work without their glasses. They may have found work but could not write and read, whether they were nearsighted or farsighted. There were lines forming in front of the store. We only let ten people in at a time to be helped and then locked the door. We could not keep up with the demand. The sign on the store read: Optician, Goldsmith, and Watchmaker. I still have the stamp showing that and stating that it was the first such facility in Sopot.

The store was on Rokossovski Street, named after a Russian marshal.[1] People said about me that I was the King Croesus[2] of all Danzig, that if I wanted I could line the entire street with twenty-dollar gold coins. I became known as the richest man in town. It was rumored that if one wanted to make money, one had just to come to our store and take care of the customers I could not take care of, since there were so many people. People also came to me to sell old currency. The reichsmark (German money used during Nazi regime) was worthless and the Polish *złotys* were issued. Stores started to sell milk and groceries, but people did not have any *złotys*, so they had to sell jewelry. I bought gold and paid in *złotys*. Our store had a separate department for those who needed reading glasses. I hired an optician from Danzig; then I added another assistant, and then I hired a watchmaker. I was doing very well.

The first elections in the Polish *Sejm* (Polish parliament) were to take place. The elections in Sopot were to be held in the building of the municipal council. They were supposed to be the first secret elections. There were two lists: List One and List Two. One of them was the extreme left; the other was more liberal and democratic, yet still Communist. The newspaper wrote that reporters from all over the world were coming to Poland to observe if the elections were being run fairly. The elections took place on a Sunday. I believe it was winter (1946) because I recall I was wearing a winter coat, and my wife wore a fur coat. I told my wife, "We have to go to vote, though neither List One nor Two reflects my views. Yet, if we don't go they will notice because I am a registered citizen and they will regard me as an enemy of the Communists, a Fascist. We have to go, but we will put in a blank ballot." I was calm about doing so because the newspapers wrote that journalists from the whole world, including America, England, and France, were here to observe the elections. So, on Sunday we went to the Municipal Council to vote. They checked their list: Białecki, Andrzej; here it was. After me, my wife's name was checked against the list. By

---

1 Note from Felicia: "Today Rokossovski Street is called Bohaterów Monte Cassino. I found it when I visited Poland in 1994."

2 Last king of Lydia renowned for his great wealth, died ca. 546 BCE.

the way, when we left our house on our way to vote, we saw groups of people holding up banners that read, "We are voting for the official list number one." There may have been two hundred factory workers who were chanting and holding up banners that said, "We are voting openly." Clerks and other citizens of Sopot marched in such a manner.

When it was our turn to cast our ballot, we saw a commission of three people sitting right by the voting urn where the voting slips are inserted. As I was about to drop my voting slip into the slot, one of the commissioners made a gesture with his hand and then covered the slit of the voting box with his hand. I made a big scene and said, "Take your paws away from the slit. Are these secret votes or forced votes?" They looked at me in astonishment and the man moved his hand away, and my wife and I placed our blank ballots into the slit. My heart was beating fast, because I realized that I was in great danger if they discovered that we inserted blank ballots. However, I made the scene knowing full well that there were reporters around, and he had no choice but to remove his hand. Only later did the consequences of my action become apparent. It was wishful thinking on my part.[3] I calmed down and forgot about the incident.

About fourteen days went by when five or six people came into my store. "We are from the Department of Revenue." And they showed me their ID. "We would like to check your books and inventory to make sure everything is in order, to make sure that all taxes were paid." I had managed my business correctly except for the incorrect things. They looked through everything; the inventory was checked and the taxes were paid.

Meanwhile, my wife became ill. She had *bazedov*, a thyroid disease (Graves' disease). She was very sick and underwent an operation on her thyroid gland. The first time she went out of the house, she came to the store and the gang from the Department of Revenue was there. She saw what was going on. Two of the investigators came up to me and said: "Listen, we know that your wife is ill. We don't want to upset her. We need the keys to your house, because we

---

3 "*Wie der kleiner Moritz sich das vorstellt.*" Literal translation: "Such as little Moritz imagines," meaning: "As I had thought so naively."

want to search it. If you don't have the keys then take them from your wife, including all the keys to all your closets."[4] I did not have the keys, and so I told my wife to give them the keys as they wanted them. I kept gold and diamonds at home, which I had bought. All of it was hidden in a secret hiding place in the desk. They went into our house and looked through everything. They got to the desk; they searched and pounded it but did not find the hiding place. My heart was in my throat as they moved the desk, checking behind it and all its drawers. They did not find anything suspicious. We went back to the store. They wrote up a report stating that all the books had been properly kept, that taxes had been paid, and the inventory had checked out with the merchandise on hand. Everything was in order. The two investigators signed off on it. I think I also signed their report. Then the gang left the store.

Not even one week later a man came to the store. My master optician was in the store helping a customer, rather than being in the workshop. We also sold eye prostheses for people who had lost an eye during the war. I had someone who made the prostheses for me and we had a selection to match it with the person. Anyway, this man came to the store, took note of the optician who happened to have a nose as used to be depicted in Streicher's newspaper (*Der Stürmer*) and went straight to him. The optician wore a white coat as was typical in an optical store. "Mr. Białecki?" he addressed the optician. "No, this is Mr. Białecki," he said, pointing at me. The man came over to me and opened a briefcase and said, "I have here a back payment of taxes due in the amount of one and a half million *złotys*. Are you going to pay it or not?" "How is that possible? The report showed everything was in order. How do you arrive at tax back payment? All my taxes were paid." "Will you pay or not? Otherwise I will have to seize your merchandise."

In order to give you an idea of what it meant to pay one and a half million *złotys*, a clerk in a high position earned at most two to three thousand *złotys* a month. I did not have one and a half million *złotys* officially in the cash register and if I had it, he would have asked me where I got this kind of money. So I said: "I am sorry, I cannot shake out one and a half million *złotys* out of my

---

4   Note from Felicia: "All closets and cabinets were kept locked to prevent the servants from stealing."

sleeve." This was more than one and a half million Belgian Francs, to put it in today's context (1981, Antwerp, Belgium).

Financially, this was not catastrophic for me, since the dollar traded for 500 *złotys* on the black market. Officially, the bank paid 4.18 *złotys* for each dollar. The man from the Department of Revenue proceeded to seal off some merchandise and said that I had to pay up within one week. Otherwise, they would remove all merchandise. After he left, I called together all my employees, the entire team. I told them to get ready to leave as I was going to the Department of Revenue. All the employees left and I locked up the door to the store. I came to the office and gave my ID to the clerk, who took it inside and out came the director of the Department of Revenue. "Oh, what an honor; Mr. Białecki himself is here. Please come in." He was very polite. "What can I do for you?" I said: "Mr. President, I came to report to you. You can arrest me; here is the key to my business. I am aware that for faulty bookkeeping you can go to jail for ten years." It was a known fact that during those days, that is in 1947, two years after the war, failure to pay taxes or keeping false books was severely punished. He said, "Dear Mr. Białecki, I cannot help you. I have no authority here; it does not come from here. The only one who can help you is the minister of finance himself in Warsaw." The minister of finance of Poland was a Jew by the name of Minz.[5] I left his office. He did not want my keys nor to arrest me. He actually had nothing to do with my situation and had nothing against me.

Only later did I realize that the majority of voters had voted for List One, because they were dependent and scared of their bosses. When I had made the scene at the poll station and the guy had withdrawn his hand from the slit in the box, he must have noted mine and my wife's name. He then later probably found the two blank ballots when counting the votes. I had a friend, a neighbor who lived on the first floor, while I lived on the second floor. His real name was Dr. Schönbach, but he had changed it to Dr. Tarczyński. He was an economist and the right hand of *Wojewoda* (county governor). We were very good friends. I told him the story and that the president of the Department of Revenue could not help me. I knew that Schönbach frequently traveled to

---

5 This could not be verified.

Warsaw on government business involving the Danzig *Wojewoda* and that he was a confidant of the government. He actually had two positions. He was also the director of the wheat commodity exchange of Gdynia, which is a town next to Danzig. He told me, "Wait, I have a very good friend who is a close friend of Minister Minz. I'll call him." Mr. Schönbach called his friend, met him, and told him that I needed his help to see the minister, since I was concerned that the minister would not meet with me otherwise. We made an appointment in a café in Warsaw, and I flew to Warsaw and met him there at an agreed time. He held a newspaper as we had planned, and we found each other right away. He was aware that he was to take me to Minister Minz, who resided at the Rewode House. He led me inside to the second floor and asked me to sit down. He went in to the minister's office and perhaps twenty minutes later, he came out. Yet instead of taking me to see the minister, he led me to the exit door and said the following: "Listen to what I have to say. The minister cannot help you. You committed an offense against the Party, and in this case, even the minister cannot help you. My best advice to you is to pay up the one and a half million *złotys* as quickly as you can and disappear from this place. If you don't get out, even after you paid the one and a half million *złotys*, two or three weeks later you'll get a payback notice for five million *złotys*. And after you pay the five million they will come back in several weeks demanding ten million. They want to ruin you. My advice is: Pay, run, and disappear."

I realized what was going on and that the ground was burning under my feet. I reported all this to Dr. Tarczyński and said to him, "I have to get out of here." He told me that he could get me in touch with a friend of his who would take me to the Belgian Consul in Warsaw. He would get me a visa. I, however, had no passport and so I had to apply for one. They summoned me to the Bespieka. It was the equivalent to the Russian NKVD.[6] The man there, who I think was Jewish, said, "You applied for a passport, Mr. Salomon Lederberger. You can receive a passport, but it will either be on the name of Lederberger, Salomon, or if you wish you must declare that you changed your name to Andrzej Białecki and officially register under that name." I flew to Kraków in

6 NKVD was the Ministry of Internal Affairs, a secret police agency equivalent to the American FBI and CIA, and a forerunner of the KGB.

order to register under the name of Andrzej Białecki, because I did not want to do so in Danzig while I still had the store. The reason was that I did not want everybody in the Danzig area to know that I was a Jew and that I lived under a false name.

In Kraków I found a private person who took care of the name change from Salomon Lederberger to Andrzej Białecki. With the "Monitor" [7] in hand, I went back to Danzig and got the passports right away. Then I went to the Belgian Consulate, which was located in the Hotel Polonia on Marszałkowska Street in Warsaw. Mr. Tarczyński's friend took me to the vice-consul, who initially demanded four hundred dollars. During these times it was prohibited to deal in dollars, even under the penalty of death. When I returned to pick up the visa, the Belgian vice-consul demanded eight hundred dollars. He had doubled his price. I asked, "How come? You had said four hundred dollars." I had no other dollars and had obtained the four hundred especially for this transaction. The vice-consul pointed to the seal and said, "I am giving you diamonds; those are diamonds. These cost eight hundred dollars." I said, "OK, but I have to get the money." I went back to the man who had brought me there and complained to him. He said that he could not do anything about it, that he was not making any money from this. He had only introduced me to the consul as a favor to Dr. Tarczyński. I asked him if he could get me the additional four hundred dollars, which he did. I went to the vice-consul with the two passports and the eight hundred dollars. I laid out the money in twenty-dollar bills on the table. The bills were a little wrinkled and the whole table was covered with twenty-dollar bills; eight hundred dollars all together. He started to yell at me, "What kind of shit is this?," and he pushed the bills off the table, which scattered all over the room. I held my breath and quickly picked up the money. It was strictly forbidden to have dollars. I had barely picked up the money from the floor when the door opened and the consul general entered. He had heard the yelling and commotion. As he came in, the vice-consul started to speak in French in a very polite manner. I did not understand French; I still don't to this day. Apparently he told the consul general that I wanted to attend a trade fair in Brussels.

---

7 Apparently the registration of a name was published in the "Monitor," which is an official registry.

It was the first trade fair after the war and I was in the diamond business and wished to attend the fair. The consul general looked at him and then at me. He said nothing, just listened as the vice-consul spoke in such a flattering way. The general consul smiled and left the room. As soon as he left, the vice-consul said, "Give me the money." He stamped the visa in our passports, signed them, and put the money in his pocket.

We were supposed to fly to Kraków and from there out of the country. The most urgent thing was to disappear from Sopot. There was a big storm. In 1947 the planes operating in Poland were small Russian planes, which had benches instead of regular seats. The flight to Kraków was to take one or one and a quarter hours. The plane kept on flying and flying. We saw something dripping out of the airplane. It was oil. Something was not right. We flew for more than two and a half hours, an hour more than was scheduled. Religious Poles in the plane started crossing themselves. Finally, the door of the cockpit opened and the stewardess came out and said we should all calm down. Unfortunately, we would not be able to land in Kraków due to the storm. Our plane had no radio contact with the ground, and Kraków was flooded. We were flying above the clouds. We were to land in Katowice, a city in Upper Silesia, which was about forty kilometers from Kraków and from there to be driven by bus to Kraków. We landed safely in Katowice. I bought a newspaper to read on the bus ride. My wife already was sitting in the bus. I sat down and saw the headlines in big print: "Belgian vice-consul shoots himself; his widow is left with six children." I again got goose bumps. I feared that the consul general probably realized what had happened in the office. Who knew if we would have problems at the Polish-Belgian border? However, we were not questioned at all at the border checkpoint.[8]

This is the end of the oral tapes with Kenneth Jacobson. Felicia Graber describes her family's subsequent years in the epilogue.

---

8   Dad adds that it can be verified that the Belgian vice-consul to Poland shot himself in 1947.

🗐 Historical Notes

Julius Streicher. Julius Streicher was the founder of *Der Stürmer*, the notoriously anti-Semitic newspaper distributed throughout the Third Reich. Born in 1885,

> *Encyclopedia Britannica* posts the following on Streicher: [Streicher] "gained infamy as one of the most virulent advocates of the persecution of Jews during the 1930s … and was a close friend of Adolf Hitler. In 1923 he founded the anti-Semitic weekly newspaper *Der Stürmer*. … *Der Stürmer*'s crude anti-Jewish invective provided a focus for Hitler's persecutory racial policies; the newspaper initiated the general campaign that led to the passage of the Nürnberg laws in 1935. … [Streicher] was captured on May 23, 1945, by U.S. troops. … [He] was found guilty on Oct. 1, 1946, of crimes against humanity and was sentenced to death by hanging."

Encyclopedia Britannica, Deluxe Edition (Chicago: Encyclopedia Britannica, 2010).

PART 2

Tosia Lederberger / Zofia Białecki

31

Mother's Story

In November 1942, after the second deportation, I went to Iwonicz with the two-and-a-half-year-old child, on Aryan papers. We were accompanied by one of our clients, engineer Pazdrów. In Iwonicz, he put me in contact with his friend who knew who I (really) was. It did not last long. I think I lived at a Mrs. Reichler's place for about two months.[1] Then, she suspected who I was (namely Jewish) and told me that she was raising my rent, and if I did not pay, she would make trouble for me. Naturally, I went to this friend (of engineer Pazdrów) and I told him what happened. He told me that I had to leave Iwonicz. I called Felicia's father in Tarnów, and he gave me the address of Zigmund Hollender in Milanówek. This man (Pazdrów's friend) helped me. He gave me (the name of) a driver who drove me in a horse-drawn wagon to the train station (to the closest town) because Iwonicz was a village (and did not have a train station). He also realized who I was and offered to drive me to Milanówek. When I arrived in Milanówek, I asked my driver to wait a few minutes. I came to Zigmund's place, and Zigmund told me that I arrived at a wrong time because the day before he had received a visit from the Polish police and he had to leave the apartment. I had travelled all night with the child, so I told him in that case, I have no alternative but to give myself up to the Gestapo because why should I suffer needlessly? If I had to perish in Tarnów, I might as well perish in Milanówek. To that Zigmund responded I should not decide so quickly; I should first dismiss the driver. I dismissed the driver. Zigmund told

---

1 We assume she sublet a room.

me that the Szpalskis were in Milanówek. (That was) Monek Szpilman, but his Aryan name was Karol Szpalski. Monek came and told me to stay, to calm down. He was going to his parents' and he would tell them about me. Half an hour later, he came back and said that he had talked to the landlady. He had told her that a cousin of his with her child was on the way to Warsaw and asked if she would allow her to spend the night in his apartment. The landlady agreed. I went to their apartment for the night. In the meantime Karol found a room for me with a railroad worker—a very decent person who worked for the *Armja Podziemnej* (underground army). I felt quite safe there. From time to time I went to the Szpalskis, the elder ones, to find out what was going on in Tarnów because Karol had connections and was able to walk around town very easily. He even managed to get me an ID card, which I myself went to the magistrate to pick up. Old man Szpilman forged a *metrika* (birth certificate) for Felicia. This (situation) also did not last long. Downstairs from us lived a lady who also had a girl Felicia's age. Once, I went out and when I came back home, this lady told me that Felicia told her that she is a Pole but really a Jewess. I was much younger in those war days naturally and had strong nerves. I took it lightly, even with a smile: "Felicia, maybe you are a Jewess or maybe you are Chinese or Greek." I took it lightly.

The next day, the landlord came to see me and told me that he knew about the incident with the child and asked me to move out. Of course I protested and showed him my papers. He told me he believed me; however, he felt sorry for me and sorry for the child, but to please look for another place to live. The next day I went again to the Szpilmans' and Karol found me a place to live, but that place did not work out. Karol had been also looking for a backup place to live, and the landlady mentioned to me that Karol must be a Jew because he is very sure of himself and has a lot of *tupek* (gall). When I heard that and told it to the Szpilmans, Karol told me that obviously I could not rent that place. Zygmunt had lived with a certain Mr. Królewski, but Zygmunt had a so-called *wsypę*.[2] Królewski, a very decent person, came to me and advised me also I should move out. He wanted to help me. He had an acquaintance, a lawyer,

---

2 The term *wsypę* refers to the Polish police coming to check on him, so that he had to move.

in Warsaw, and I could work as his maid. He wanted to place the child in a children's home where she could sleep. He even tried to get a bed for the child. I did not go along with that because I did not want to separate from the child. I said, "Whatever will be with me, will be with the child. I want to be with the child."

Karol went to Warsaw, and when he returned, he said that in Warsaw two women from Tarnów had a room on Szucha 11, and they could take me in. So I packed up and went to Warsaw with the child. By the way, the next day, Zygmunt's wife, Helenka, came to me and told me, "You ran away from the grave digger's shovel. The landlord denounced you and they were looking for the lady with the child with black hair and long braids."
 In Warsaw I lived with the two women ("the sisters"). It was not bad. In that house, there also lived Poles who had children. I had to let the child go out to the garden to play because it would have been suspicious if I did not let her go downstairs. Whenever she went down, I took *brom* (a tranquilizer) to calm down. I taught her the Lord's Prayer and she wore a pendant of Holy Mother, which was from our store.[3]

Various people from Tarnów would come to our place, and we found out that there had been a third deportation and that nobody was left in the ghetto. I thought that Schlomek was no more. I even went to a psychic and showed her a picture of Schlomek. She told me that that person had perished recently by Hitler's hand. Naturally, I was very desperate because I remained alone in the world with the child. I also had no means to live on, just a little jewelry. Once every two weeks Marian Urban had come from Tarnów.[4] Urban was a simple man, an acquaintance, and always brought me some money. When he did not come two weeks later, I saw this as a sign that he had nothing to bring me.

One day, he came with my husband, who arrived in a railroad worker's uniform, but he could not show himself to the neighbors. He sat behind the

---

3 Felicia still has this pendant.
4 Marian Urban was a farmer, an acquaintance of our parents who served as a messenger between Mother and Father as long as he was in the ghetto. He was the only one who knew Mother's address in Warsaw. Father did not want to know it for security reasons. Marian is the one who accompanied Father to Warsaw.

wardrobe. I put the heavy wardrobe catty-corner.[5] Times were very difficult because our lives lay in the hands of this child. Whenever she would go down to play, I reminded her twenty times that she lived only with me in the room, no one else. She was already so well trained that when I woke her at night and asked her, "Felusju, who do you live with?" the child would tell me—she was three at the time—"Mother, I already know everything. Please let me sleep." At night, I made her say the Lord's Prayer and kneel. I went to church with her almost every Sunday. When Easter came I went to church to have the eggs blessed. She was the first to run up and kneel by the altar and pray. She was a real Catholic.

It was difficult. Once the landlord of the lodging came to us and said that a neighbor noticed a black-haired girl and that that must be a Jewess. The landlord was a very decent man. He threatened the neighbor that if "a hair fell off the woman or that child's head" (if anything bad should happen to them), she would pay for it. Once, after this incident, we were sitting in the room and someone knocked. Of course, I shut the child up; I held the child's mouth so that she would not talk. We pretended that nobody was home. We were afraid that the Gestapo had come to get us. Someone knocked a few times. Finally that person left. We thought that the Gestapo was looking for us. We had a backup place, but when we got to that apartment, the owner was not there. I do not remember anymore what happened—if we stayed there, if we slept there or not. In any case we returned to our room on Szucha Street.

In 1944 the Warsaw Uprising broke out; that is when we left everything and moved. Schlomek buried a few personal belongings. And we walked and walked until we got to Pruszków, to the camp. In Pruszków, they separated the men from the women. It was a terrible night, and we lay in mud. The child slept on the small suitcase, and then my husband somehow managed to get to us and he had his hand in a sling, as if he were sick and could not go to work to Germany. But despite that, I left earlier with the child, because women with children up to two years could leave to freedom; the rest had to go to work.

---

5 As explained earlier, Father had to hide as he could not live officially anywhere as this would neces-sitate registering with the Polish authority. This was too dangerous as his papers indicated that he was a silk merchant and he wore a railroad worker uniform. Furthermore, his Polish was not perfect, as was that of many Polish Jews.

As Felicia was not tall and almost looked like a two-year-old, I managed to get out with her, to freedom. I was free and walked with a neighbor, a certain Dąbrowska, who also had a little boy[6]. We walked in the countryside from hut to hut and we spent nights in stables. We walked aimlessly because we had no place to stay and we did not know what was going on.

We were walking and we saw an electric train that went from village to village. I got on that train and my husband walked in. Naturally, we were very happy. Of course, Felicia did not know that it was her father. I had told her that it was an uncle. In front of the neighbors I was the wife of an officer, my husband was in the war, and I did not know anything about his whereabouts. When we got off the train, and as we were walking, we met a man from Tarnów, Pelek Perlberger. He told us that we could find shelter in this particular village. And in fact, we found shelter. First, we stayed with one peasant, but that did not work out, because he was a very mean person. Later, we came across others, the Sierocińskis. Of course they did not know that we were Jews. They were very nice, especially to the child. Each Sunday they killed a chicken; they always gave her some of it to eat. That is how we somehow managed on Aryan papers. On the fifteenth of January, 1945, we were liberated. The Russians entered Warsaw. In Chyliczki, where we lived, the Russians showed up on January 18.

I forgot to tell about an incident I had, when I was in Chyliczki. Every week I went to Grodzisk, a small town, to the market, of course on foot. Of course, I went alone. And one time, there was a roundup of women to take them to work to Germany. A few other women and I hid on a roof, and instead of coming home at noon I got home in the afternoon. It is difficult to describe today my feelings and my fears. With whom would my child stay and how would she manage? How desperate the child must be not knowing where her mother was. That is how we somehow survived this war.

After the eighteenth of January, 1945, my husband walked to Warsaw in the hope of perhaps finding some of our things, but he returned with nothing. In the meantime, the money became devalued. I was actually starving. Even for money the peasants did not want to give up a potato. I had a friend, a Pole; I

---

6 Felicia remembers playing with a little boy in the cellar during bombing attacks on Warsaw during the uprising.

cannot think of her name right now. I went to her. She had a son. Her husband, a Jew, had been killed. Whatever her child ate she shared with my child. When my husband came back from Warsaw with nothing, we took off on an open freight train and went to Łódź. In Łódź, we were supposedly free, but we were still called Białecki.

We remained on Aryan papers after liberation because we heard that in Kraków and in Kielce and some other places, there were incidents of shooting Jews. So, we stayed on Aryan papers. I stayed with the little one in Łódź; we lived on the sixth floor. It was very difficult. Then the child became very sick. In the meantime, my husband went to Sopot. He managed to go to Sopot because we had to find a way to live. He went to Sopot, and then I was alone for a few months or a few weeks, I do not remember. Then, I went together with another woman to Sopot. In Sopot, life was more or less normal. We remained on the Aryan papers. But then there were Russians and I did not want to stay in Poland. In the meantime, my son was born in 1946. All along Felicia thought that Andrzej was not her father, and when soldiers were returning from the war, she kept telling me, "Mother, come. Maybe Father will come back."

I won't tell details, how we got the passports. That is not important, and besides I do not remember a lot of things. Soon after we came to Sopot I paid a steep price,; I was sick with *bazedov* (Graves' disease), which I still feel to this day. From Sopot we went to Brussels and only then did Father reveal to Felicia how we survived the war.

And so life went on, and we struggled like this even after the war, like everyone. We were running, trying to start life anew. It is very possible that I omitted a lot of things because, in the meantime, I went through a lot of illnesses, and so I described only in broad terms how I survived the war with my child.

 **Epilogue**

Our mother's narrative deals mainly with the years she spent alone with me in Warsaw, and our father's account ends with our escape from Poland in 1947. Our family's history, however, does not end that year of course. We lived in Brussels, Belgium, until 1951, years that were very difficult for both our parents.

Before leaving Poland, Father had exchanged as much cash as he could from Polish *złotys* to British pounds as these were deemed more valuable. After arriving in Brussels, he found out that they were all forged bills. In 1942, the Germans had set up counterfeit "Operation Bernhard" using prisoners to print British pounds in order to undermine the British economy.[1] Unaware of this, Father had bought those worthless bills; the result being that we were quite destitute. Father needed to work to support us, but, although the Belgian government was willing to give us political asylum, it refused to issue work permits to any foreigner. Thus Father was forced to find other avenues to make a living. He went to Frankfurt, Germany, then under United States occupation, where there was complete freedom to set up any business. For four long years, he commuted the five-hundred-mile round-trip trek once a week.

Mother, again, was left to her own devices in a foreign country, not speaking the language, having to make due with a meager income and having to care for my toddler brother, born June 1946 in Sopot, and me. Again and again,

---

1 More information on Operation Bernhard can be found on the following websites: http://www. lawrencemalkin.com/index.html and http://www.post-gazette.com/pg/07022/755902-28.stm.

Mother refused to move the family to Germany, saying, "I will not raise my children on German soil!"

Finally, however, in 1951, she relented and we relocated to Frankfurt. I got married to a United States Army chaplain in December 1959, and our parents, together with my brother, returned to Belgium in 1961. As a result, Leon lived in three different countries, learned three different languages, and had attended seven different schools by the time he arrived in the United States for college at the age of eighteen. My husband and I came to the States in 1963 with our two young children.

By 1989, Father was not well; Mother could not cope alone, so we, Leon and I, brought our parents to St. Louis where we both live. Father died in 1991 and Mother in 1993. In my book, *Amazing Journey: Metamorphosis of a Hidden Child* (2010), I recount, from my perspective and in more details, the story of our lives until 2006, the year I was bestowed the Woman of Valor award from my congregation Nusach Hari B'Nai Zion.

—Felicia Graber

Acknowledgments

This book would not have been possible without the twelve-hour taped interview that author Kenneth Jacobson recorded with our father, Salomon Lederberger. Mr. Jacobson's patience, friendly attitude, and open-ended questioning during the interviews elicited a glut of memories that are the backbone of this memoir. My husband and I had the privilege of meeting Mr. Jacobson and were deeply impressed by his devotion to the topic of the impact the Holocaust had on survivors. Our children, grandchildren, and future generations will benefit from Mr. Jacobson's work. It brings insight into the difficult living conditions during the Nazi occupation of Poland, the struggles for survival, and the amazing courage of our parents. We owe an enormous debt of gratitude to Mr. Jacobson for giving this precious gift to our family.

My friend Felicia Wertz spent hours researching historical facts that needed corroboration, rectifying the Polish spelling of proper names, cities, and streets, and transcribing and translating our mother's Polish oral history tape. Her contribution to this volume is extremely valuable.

My friend, mentor, and teacher, Bobbi Linkemer, has always stood by my side. Her encouragement and prompting made my book *Amazing Journey: Metamorphosis of a Hidden Child* become a reality. Her insights, suggestions, questioning, and editing of this volume helped make it more readable and understandable.

Dan Reich, Curator and Director of Education at the St. Louis Holocaust Museum and Learning Center, spent hours reading this material and making suggestions. His insights have been invaluable in helping clarify issues that evolved in the context of the narration. I deeply value Mr. Reich's friendship and encouragement in all my endeavors.

I greatly appreciate the patience and the talent of the creator of the cover and layout, Peggy Nehmen. It is a pleasure to work with her. She is always willing to accommodate, and her subtle suggestions are always on the mark.

Katherine Pickett, our copyeditor's guidance was invaluable, especially in the help she gave me as far as the correct way notations in the historical notes should be handled. She spent hours checking my information, making changes how my sources were listed and advising me on the acceptable rules of quoting published material. I am very grateful for her assistance.

A special "thank you" to the Holocaust Education & Archive Research Team (H.E.A.R.T), www.holocaustresearchproject for their very gracious permission to use any material from their website.

Last, but certainly not least, Leon and I want to thank our respective spouses and families for their understanding, support, and patience during the long hours we spent on this project.

This project would have never been accomplished without the help of everyone mentioned above.

—Felicia Graber

About the Authors

Dr. Leon Bialecki was born in Sopot, Poland in June of 1946. He immigrated to the USA at the age of 18; by then he had lived in three different countries, learned three different languages and had attended seven different schools. He studied medicine at Washington University School of Medicine, graduating in 1972 and spent twenty years as director of an Intensive Care Unit at Christian North East Hospital in St. Louis, Missouri. Dr. Bialecki lives in St Louis, with his wife Ilana. They have two sons, Dr. Eldad Bialecki and Dr. Daniel Bialecki and two grandsons.

Felicia Lederberger-Bialecki-Graber, a retired teacher from the Parkway School District, is a docent and speaker at the St Louis Holocaust Museum and Learning Center. She speaks about the Holocaust in area colleges, schools, and community agencies. Felicia's book, *Amazing Journey, Metamorphosis of a Hidden Child* was published in 2010, and she is a contributor to the anthology; *And Life is Changed Forever,* published by Wayne University Press, 2006. Felicia's writings have also been published in magazines and newsletters nation-wide. The founder of the St. Louis Survivors and Descendants of the Holocaust, she lives in St. Louis with her husband, Rabbi Howard Graber. They have two children, eight grandchildren and one great-grandchild.

Family picture taken before the war ca.1937/38 probably in Tarnów.
We do not know the names of everyone in the photograph.

1) Paternal grandfather, Leib Israel Lederberger
2) Our paternal grandmother Sarah Rosenzweig-Lederberger
3) Uncle Adolf Rosenzweig, grandmother's brother
4) Our father, Salomon Lederberger
5) Tadek Brand, Father's cousin
6) Lina Rosenzweig, Adolf's wife
7) Rachel Kresch, Father's sister

Father's sister and parents: Rachel Kresch, Sarah and Leib Israel Lederberger.

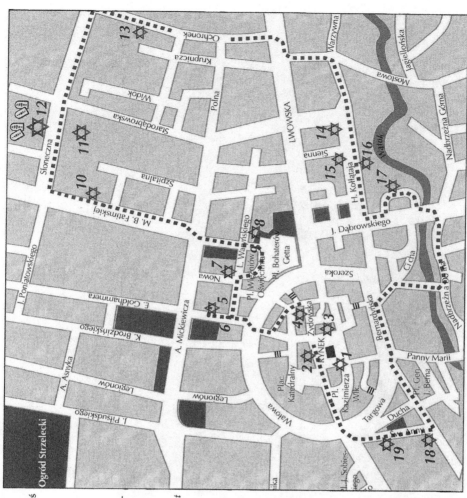

1. Rynek City-square
2. Muzeum Okręgowe Regional Museum
3. Najstarsza część miasta zamieszkana niegdyś przez Żydów
   The oldest part of the city where Jews used to live
4. Bima – pozostałość po najstarszej bóżnicy żydowskiej
   Bimah – the remnants of an old Jewish synagogue
5. Budynek Żydowskiego Towarzystwa Kredytowego
   The building of the Jewish Credit Association
6. Ocalały fragment napisu reklamującego dania restauracyjne
   A preserved part of a sign advertising restaurant dishes
7. Tu stała synagoga Nowa
   The New Synagogue used to stand here
8. Budynek byłej mykwy – żydowskiej łaźni rytualnej
   The building of an old mikveh – a ritual Jewish bath
9. Pomnik I Transportu Więźniów do Oświęcimia
   A monument commemorating the first nazi transportation of prisoners to Auschwitz
10. Żydowski Dom Starców
    Jewish home for the aged
11. Szpital żydowski Jewish hospital
12. Cmentarz żydowski Jewish cemetery
13. Dom Robotniczy Workers' House
14. Żydowski Dom Sierot Jewish orphanage
15. Szkoła Talmud Tora "Talmud Tora" School
16. Młyn H. Szancera H. Szancer's mill
17. Szkoła Jawne "Jawne" School
18. Tu stała synagoga reformowana – Tempel
    Reformed synagogue – "Tempel" was located here
19. Szkoła Stowarzyszenia Safa Berura
    School of "Safa Berura" Society

Map of Tarnów Ghetto
© *In the Footsteps of the Jews of Tanów*, Adam Bartosz, Regional Museum of Tarnów, 2nd edition 2002.

Leah Blumenkrantz and her mother Estera Blumenkrantz (Mother's friend).
Far right is Mother with Felicia, approximately 18 months old, in Tarnów, Poland.

The Michalewicz House, Tarnów, we lived upstairs.

Announcement

Beginning on September 10, 1942, evacuations of the Jews will take place.

- Any Pole interfering in any way will be severely punished.
- Any Pole providing a hiding place or shelter to a Jew during this operation, will be shot.
- Entry permits to the Jewish residential quarter are cancelled as of publication of this notice.
- Anyone who enters the ghetto in spite of this, will be severely punished and risks being shot.
- Anyone who directly or indirectly purchases property or equipment from a Jew, or comes to own such property as a gift or in any way, will be severely punished.
- Any Pole in possession of Jewish property or goods, must notify the Security Police headquarters in Tarnow; anyone who does not, will be severely punished as a looter.
- During the transport of the Jews from the assembly point to the railway station, access to the following streets and square is forbidden.

Lwowska St, Bernardynska St, Stary Rynek, Ogrodowa St., Narutowicza St., Bandrowskiego St., and Plac Sportowy. As the transport approaches, residents must lock their doors and windows, and are forbidden to observe the transport. Noncompliance will be punished.

September 9, 1942

Der Kreishauptmann
Dr. PERNUTZ

The second deportation. This is a reproduction of the announcement posted in the Tarnów ghetto decreeing the second deportation, now displayed in the Jewish Historical Institute in Warsaw.

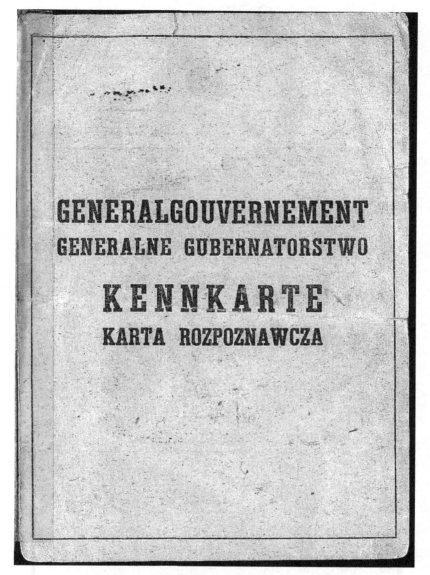

Front of Polish ID card obtained before we left the ghetto.

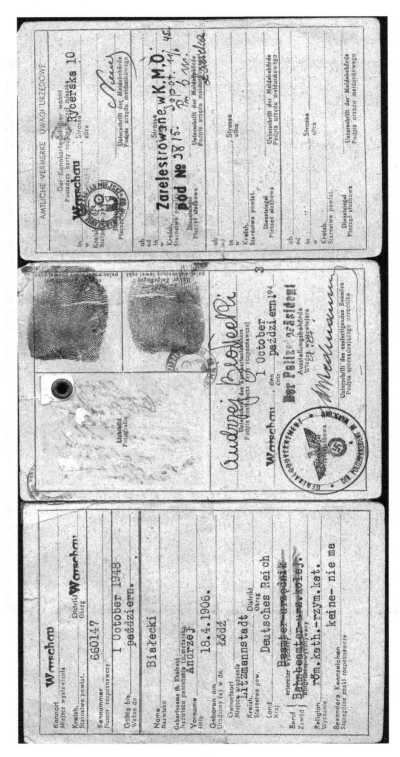

Father's Aryan ID card as Andrzej Białecki, inside view, his photo is missing.

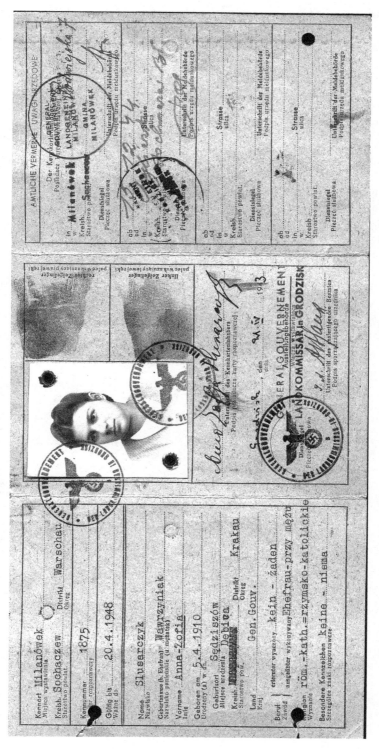

Mother's Aryan ID card, inside view.

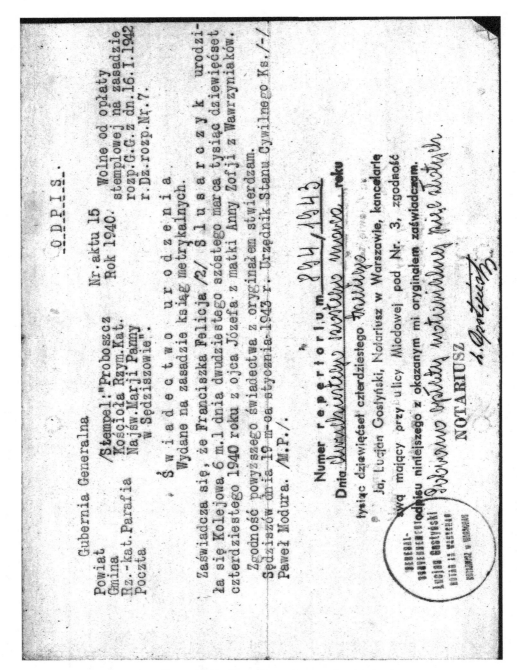

"Notarized" copy of Felicia's forged Aryan birth certificate.

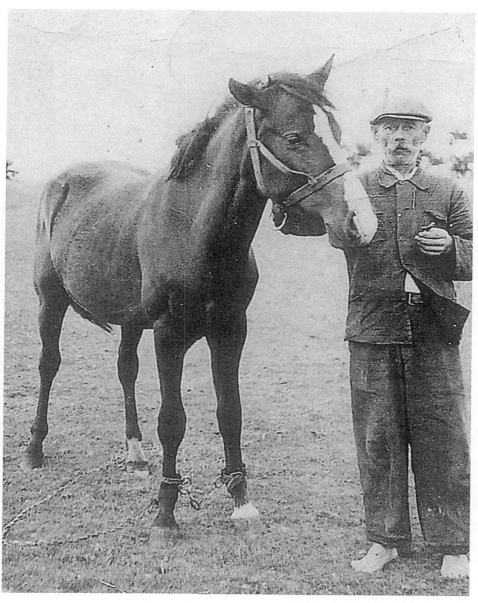

Piotr Sierociński, the peasant who sheltered us, Chyliczki, Poland.

Eleanore Sierociński, Piotr's wife, Chyliczki, Poland.

Zarząd Miejski m. Sopotu

Nr. dz. x/2347

dnia 22. października 1945.

Karta rzemieślnicza Nr. 112

wydana na podstawie art. 147 Rozp. Prezydenta Rzeczypospolitej z dnia 7. 6. 1927 r. (Dz. Ust. Nr. 53)
w brzmieniu ustawy z dnia 10. 3. 1934 r. (Dz. Ust. Nr. 40 poz. 350) na skutek zgłoszenia z dnia

Białeckiemu Andrzejowi

Ob.

Obywatelowi   polskiemu

Urodzonemu dnia   18.4.1906.   w Łodzi

na prowadzenie rzemiosła   zegarmistrzowsko-jubilerskiego.

w   Sopocie przy ul. Rokossowskiego 25

przez zastępcę

pod firmą   Białecki Andrzej

Uwagi: na mocy nabyte zgodnie z art. 158 z dnia 7.6.1927.

Za Prezydenta
Nacz. Oddz. Przem.

podpis
/Inż. Majewski./

License to open a watchmaker/jewelry store in Sopot, Poland,
dated October 22, 1945.

Felicia with Mother on the pier in Sopot, Poland, ca. 1945.

From left, Father, Mother, Felicia, Marian Urban, the messenger who helped us.
Sopot, Poland, ca. 1945.

Father on the pier in Sopot, Poland, ca. 1946.

Mother on the pier in Sopot, Poland, ca.1946.

Father with Leon in Brussels, Belgium, ca. 1947.

Mother with Leon, Brussels, Belgium, ca. 1947.

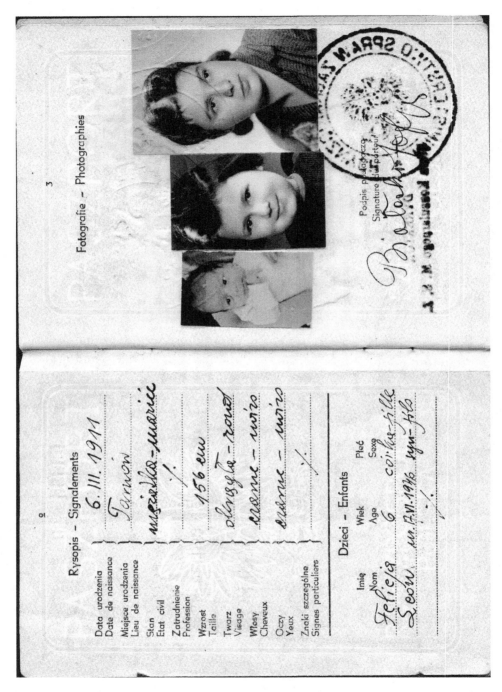

The inside of Mother's Polish passport. From left to right: Leon, Felicia, and Mother.

Visa to Belgium, stamped in Polish Passport, issued 1947.

Salomon and Tosia Lederberger-Bialecki at grandson's wedding, November 5, 1985.
Baltimore, Maryland

Made in the USA
Middletown, DE
23 July 2023